D1058586

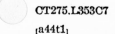

ALEXANDER LEGGE

1866–1933

DEEPTONE REPRODUCTION FROM A PAINTING BY JEAN WHITE

Alexander Legge

1866–1933

ALEXANDER LEGGE

1866–1933

The life story of a truly great American who loved and served his country well, who achieved world-wide distinction as an industrial leader, as a patriotic public servant and as the devoted friend and champion of all who till the soil

By Forrest Crissey

PRIVATELY PRINTED AT CHICAGO, ILLINOIS
IN 1936 BY THE ALEXANDER LEGGE
MEMORIAL COMMITTEE

B

FOREWORD

BY SAM R. McKELVIE, *Chairman of*
The Alexander Legge Memorial Committee

Wʜᴇɴ *this volume has been published and dis-
tributed the purpose for which our Committee
was formed will have been accomplished. That
purpose was not merely to pay further tribute to one who had
already been widely honored in life and at his death; it was
also to make available for this generation and for posterity—
and particularly for the youth of this and other lands—a faithful and intimate life story of a truly great American about
whom strangely little was known, considering the world-wide
eminence he had attained.*

*The carrying out of this purpose has been a labor of love
and pride to those concerned in it. Frankly, I was glad indeed
to accept the chairmanship of the Memorial Committee because
of my intimate acquaintance and close friendship with Alex
Legge, my association with him in public service, and my affectionate admiration of his personality and character. Now it is
my further privilege to set forth in these lines some account of
the Memorial Committee, its plans and its work.*

*Very soon after Alex Legge's death on December 3, 1933,
suggestions from various sources made it seem that there was a
spontaneous and general desire that his life and labors should*

be enduringly commemorated. It was not until about a year later, however, that this desire developed into the movement out of which came the formation of the Memorial Committee. The credit for this development belongs chiefly to Guy L. Noble, who was the prime mover in bringing the Committee together and who, as Executive Secretary, has contributed most importantly to such success as the Committee has achieved.

Let it be noted here that in some sense the Memorial Committee and its work, including this volume, are a by-product of the great 4-H Club movement in which Alex Legge's far-visioned mind foresaw, while the movement was still in its infancy, one of the most potent forces for the advancement of American agriculture. As Managing Director of the National Committee on Boys and Girls Club Work, Mr. Noble has organized the constructive individual and industrial activities in that field and co-ordinated them with the program of the Agricultural Colleges and United States Department of Agriculture in carrying forward the 4-H movement to its present high place in the nation.

Mr. Legge's early recognition of this new factor in the country's agricultural and rural life, followed by his acceptance of a 4-H directorship, brought these two men together in a relationship which amply explains Mr. Noble's inspiration and energy in securing the formation of the Memorial Committee and his active interest in its work.

The response to letters inviting a limited list of Mr. Legge's most intimate associates and friends to join the Memorial Committee was instant and unanimous. As Mr. Noble has told me, "the Alexander Legge Memorial Committee seemed to have been organized almost overnight." Fortunately, George A. Ranney, who had been for many years an intimate associate of Alex Legge in the management of the International Harvester Company, consented to act as treasurer of the Committee.

Early in its deliberations the Memorial Committee reached some definite conclusions. It was decided that Mr. Legge's life and work could be best commemorated by a competent biography; that there should be in addition provision for three portraits done in oil; and that the Committee's work should be privately underwritten without solicitation of funds. One of the portraits hangs in the gallery of the Saddle and Sirloin Club; another is in the Agricultural Building of the University of Wisconsin, the state of Alex Legge's birth; and the third occupies a place of honor in the Agricultural College of the University of Nebraska, the state where he spent so many years of his life and where he began his business career.

Another conclusion of the Memorial Committee was that the biography should be a simple, straight-forward narrative in keeping with the character and the ways of the man whose life it was to portray; that it should be an undocumented biography, because Alex Legge was so notably an undocumented man—a man of action rather than words; one little given to making speeches or being interviewed, seldom revealing his inner self in correspondence or conversation.

Because of his ability and reputation as a writer, his experience, patience and skill in biographical research, and his long acquaintance with Alex Legge, the task of authorship was entrusted to Forrest Crissey. No limitations or restrictions were laid upon him. The Memorial Committee's sole sugges-

tion was that the biography should be an appreciation rather than an appraisal; that it should not be sheerly eulogistic, but should present a very great and intensely human man in sympathetic but realistic terms, revealing him in the lights and shadows wherein he was seen by those who had witnessed his career from boyhood to the grave. How well Mr. Crissey performed his task is sufficiently evidenced by the book itself.

S. R. McK.

Lincoln, Nebraska

THE ALEXANDER LEGGE
MEMORIAL COMMITTEE

SAM R. McKELVIE, *Chairman*
GEORGE A. RANNEY, *Treasurer*
GUY L. NOBLE, *Executive Secretary*

PHILIP D. ARMOUR	A. E. McKINSTRY
C. S. BATTLE	D. R. McLENNAN
C. H. BURLINGAME	EUGENE MEYER
CHARLES HENRY BUTLER	GEORGE S. MILNOR
RICHARD CAMPBELL	ARTHUR F. MULLEN
CHRIS L. CHRISTENSEN	FRANK E. MULLEN
E. F. CREEKMORE	EDWARD A. O'NEAL
CHARLES G. DAWES	BURTON F. PEEK
PAUL A. DRAPER	GEORGE N. PEEK
CHARLES A. EWING	R. C. POLLOCK
F. D. FARRELL	GEORGE L. RICE
CHAS. K. FOSTER	HENRY M. ROBINSON
JAMES H. GORE	A. R. ROGERS
CLIFFORD V. GREGORY	DANIEL C. ROPER
HERBERT J. HODGE	T. A. RUSSELL
DR. DAYTON B. HOLCOMB	W. F. SCHILLING
HERBERT HOOVER	C. H. SCHWEPPE
CLARK HOWELL	ARCH W. SHAW
ARTHUR M. HYDE	E. S. SIMPSON
C. T. JAFFRAY	T. G. STALLSMITH
GEORGE R. JAMES	JAMES C. STONE
HUGH S. JOHNSON	JOHN STUART
HORACE C. KLEIN	GERARD SWOPE
THOMAS W. LAMONT	L. J. TABER
FRANK O. LOWDEN	SAMUEL M. VAUCLAIN
GEORGE MacDONALD	C. C. WEBBER
A. R. MANN	SANFORD B. WHITE
CYRUS H. McCORMICK	DR. WM. A. WHITE
HAROLD F. McCORMICK	EDWARD FOSS WILSON
E. B. McGUINN	CLARENCE M. WOOLLEY

OWEN D. YOUNG

CONTENTS

Contents

LIST OF ILLUSTRATIONS

Alexander Legge's Scottish Background and Ancestry

FOLLOWING the trail of Alexander Legge from his birth on a Wisconsin farm, the year after the Civil War, to his international recognition as one of the greatest industrial and economic leaders produced under the American system of "rugged individualism" has been a thrilling quest. Early in that search, however, it became impressively clear that the foundations of his character and characteristics were laid many years before, back in stony Scotland, by strong men and women who lived hard, self-reliant lives, whose mental and moral fiber, like their muscles, was toughened by unceasing and valiant struggles with granite obstacles and conditions.

Few Americans of distinction have more logically carried forward the trends of their ancestors than Alexander Legge. He so definitely reflected and developed his family background that some knowledge of his forebears, the Legges and the Frasers, is vital to an understanding of how this farm boy, with an education of no more than a few terms in school, came to have a mind of such penetrative and constructive power that he proved himself a

match for European premiers and diplomats in many of
the most complex and important economic adjustments
incident to the World War and its problems. His gift
of hard common sense, of sound practical judgment,
amounted to genius.

Any attempt to account for Alex Legge without examination of his ancestral stock would be contrary to his
strongest family traditions. He himself definitely recognized his debt to the long line of Alexander Legges running back to the days of "Bonnie Prince Charlie," for on
his visit to Scotland he hunted out records and living
relatives holding the secrets of his clan.

This quest did not have the usual objective of estab-
lishing connection with aristocratic families or illustrious
persons. He was not interested in proving his right to an
ancestral coat-of-arms. Possibly no other American placed
less value upon social rank. This indifference to kinship
with titled aristocracy is pointedly indicated by the fact
that he dismissed the English Legges without a flicker of
interest. Thomas Legge, who lived in Kent in the reign
of Edward III, was the direct ancestor of the Earls of
Dartmouth, was twice Lord Mayor of London, married
the daughter of the Earl of Harwick, and lent substantial
sums to his sovereign. He spelled his name "Legge." But
he was English, so Alex Legge summarily dismissed him
from consideration. Subconsciously, perhaps, his objective in "rummaging about Scotland" was to gain an understanding of the kind of persons who had passed on to
him their physical and mental traits.

This, however, states his interest in those researches
rather too rigidly. He was naturally an ardent clansman
and his sense of family attachments was unusually strong.
Those nearest in the line had been known and loved by

his father and mother who had told him, as a child, of their traits and experiences. The Legges and the Frasers in this austere ancestral procession were his own people and consequently they commanded his spontaneous and sympathetic interest on the ground of kinship.

In the course of his quest he encountered tales of an early ancestor who, according to family tradition, met his death at the hands of a public executioner. In discussing this unhappy incident with an old Scotchman, Alex Legge advanced the theory that this was probably due to over-zealous devotion to the fortunes of "Bonnie Prince Charlie." With twinkling and mischievous eyes his informant replied:

"Na! I think it had t' do wi' sheep!"

This incident delighted Alex Legge and he often related it with great relish which, of course, he would not have done had his investigations of the family tree been dictated by the usual pride of ancestry. He made no effort to hide the actual or legendary black sheep of the family flock; they interested him quite as much as the members of the clan whose reputations were as immaculate as that of Dr. James Legge who made one of the earliest translations of the Bible into the Chinese language while a missionary in that country.

He was not especially thrilled by this pious achievement, nor even by the discovery that the mother of Lord Byron was his grandmother's cousin. Had this relationship to his line run to Robert Burns, his pride would have been immense, for the songs of the humble Scottish bard were Alex Legge's literary Bible, and he had most of them at his tongue's end. This was equally true of his father. They both regarded Robbie Burns as the world's greatest master of the secrets of human nature.

Alexander Legge, "Old Sandy," father of Alex, named his Nebraska home farm for the original family estate a short distance out of Inverurie, Aberdeenshire, Scotland.

Driving along a road commanding an impressive view of Benache Mountain and its foothills, one might easily pass by the Aberdeenshire estate without observing the entrance to the driveway leading through carefully tended grounds up to a two-story house built of the white granite so generally used in that section.

Especially in his later years, Old Sandy often remarked that if this ancient family seat of the Legge clan had not been confiscated by George II, the Hanoverian king of England, in a determination to suppress the Scottish clans and punish those who participated in the futile "Bonnie Prince Charlie" uprising of 1745, he would himself have been Laird of "Leggett's Den." The Scottish use of the word "den" implies a cozy and secluded retreat rather than a lair of wild beasts.

Family interest and pride in "Leggett's Den" have persisted from one generation of Legges to another with peculiar vitality. When Old Sandy bought a place of his own in Nebraska, he planted a double row of trees from the house out to the public road, after the landscape pattern of the old family seat at Inverurie. To his granddaughter, Ina Sharman, he once remarked, not long after the trees were planted:

"Some day their branches will meet over our drive as they do over the driveway leading into Leggett's Den, back in Scotland."

Shortly after the funeral of Old Sandy, his daughter, Christina Sharman, said to her daughter Ina:

"I noticed as the hearse went down the drive that the branches of the trees met above it. Your grandfather lived to see this wish fulfilled, and it pleased him greatly in his last days to look up at the leafy arch that spanned the private driveway."

There was, it eventually developed, another and a more personal reason for the peculiar interest which the father of Alex Legge had in Leggett's Den of Aberdeenshire. This family secret did not come definitely into the open until 1912, when Christina Legge Sharman, the eldest of Old Sandy's children, revisited the land of her birth with her husband and daughter.

Although only four years old when taken to America, she retained vivid recollections of Scotland. These memories were tinged with the glamour of a child's viewpoint. Besides, it seemed to her that she knew the relatives back home almost as intimately as if she had lived with them throughout her years in America, for her mother had talked of them eagerly and tirelessly. These family sagas were Tena's bedtime stories. She possessed not only the Legge characteristic of an extremely retentive memory but also a romantic imagination and an irrepressible sense of humor.

While visiting in the home of Ellen and George Smith, whose father was half-brother to Christina Fraser Legge, Old Sandy's romantic secret was unexpectedly disclosed. Cousin Ellen was a forthright person who spoke her mind fearlessly and without reserve.

"Your mother," she abruptly declared to Christina, "was the countryside beauty, and could 'a had onyone she wanted—even the Laird whom my father wanted her to take—but she took the worst of the lot!"

Then the daughter of "the worst of the lot" of her mother's suitors had her high moment of frankness and pride, and she made the most of her opportunity. This revelation of her mother's romance was, however, more in the nature of a confirmation of a girlhood impression than a surprise, for she recalled that occasionally she had heard her father teasingly rally her mother with the question: "An' mebbe now ye wish ye had taken the Laird?" This had not meant much to her at the time, but now it took on revealing definiteness.

Pride had always been accounted a deadly sin in the stern decalogue of Christina Sharman and her people, but for once she shamelessly indulged this forbidden frailty and made a masterful job of it in defense of her mother and father. She well understood the high estimate placed by the Scots upon material property and worldly success. The lass who married property married well, unless she took a husband who was "irreligious," a rogue, or one maliciously unkind to his family. Calmly, judicially, Christina gave the kinswoman who had expressed so poor an opinion of her father a detailed inventory of the property accumulations of the daring Sandy who had "cut out" the Laird—so many hundred acres of rich land, so many hundred cattle, and so many thousand dollars left to his children.

Christina's daughter, who gleefully overheard this recital of Sandy's achievements, later remarked: "Mother, you left out nothing but the cat. And did you notice Cousin Ellen's eyes growing bigger with each added item?"

Then came the verdict of the amazed Ellen, who apparently had been making rapid mental calculations comparing Sandy's property accumulations with those of the rejected Laird: "Well, he did better than most."

And Sandy, with his keen, whimsical wit, his sparkling sense of fun and his unfailing gentleness to his "Kirstie",

"ALEXANDER THE MILLER"
GRANDFATHER OF ALEX

NEW MILL, INVERURIE, ABERDEENSHIRE, SCOTLAND

had held her devoted love through many lean, hard years of pioneering. True, he caused her to miss becoming mistress of a Scottish estate, but eventually he enabled her to preside over property even more extensive in Nebraska.

Alex Legge never failed to recognize the fact that both his father and mother were persons of exceptional mental force and character. He was proud of them, particularly of their remarkable business judgment—a quality which they shared almost equally. Repeatedly he remarked to his intimates that his father never made a business move of any importance without consulting his wife and that her judgment generally determined his action. This, he observed, was characteristic of the Legge men. They made their wives full business partners, and with good reason, for they married keen women. After his own marriage he followed the traditional family practice of taking his wife into full confidence as to his personal business affairs. They "pulled together," to use his own expression.

In the ancestral background of Alex Legge the figure of a remarkable woman stands out with sharp distinctness—his Legge grandmother, wife of "Alexander the Miller." Even in Scotland, where rugged individuality was and still is common among women, this mother of Old Sandy was accounted a "character" of the most pronounced type. Her ruling passion was for cattle raising. Not only did she transmit this predilection to her son, Sandy, but she developed it as devotedly as if it had involved his soul's salvation. When he was just emerging from childhood she took him regularly to the cattle markets and the fairs, leading him from one creature to another, patiently explaining the good points or the defects of each animal. Usually this involved "feeling" the creatures.

"Put your hand here, Sandy," she would say. "There's the spot that'll tell if the yearling will make a fine animal that'll please the judges. Aye, an' here's anither spot that has muckle to tell if only your fingers can learn how to read it. It's not so easy to get wisdom into your fingertips; but it'll come, Sandy. When ye're in doot, feel the best animal and then the worst. That'll teach ye!"

Mostly the cattle in the market stalls and the show pens which they industriously frequented were fine Aberdeen Angus stock, for here was the home of this proud and hardy breed. Mother and son wasted little time on the rougher breeds that occasionally found their way into the markets and fairs from the Highlands. The aristocrats of Aberdeenshire virtually monopolized their attention.

The lad responded eagerly to this intensive training in the art of judging cattle. He was foreordained by the iron will of his mother to become a "greve" or stock farm manager. This was the career for her son, and she was determined that he should be well prepared to make good in it.

Alexander the Miller, grandfather of Alex, lived at Mill of Bruxie, Old Deer, Aberdeenshire, and it was here that Sandy, the father of Alex, was born January 27, 1829, "at three o'clock in the morning" as runs the birth record. The miller was in comfortable circumstances in the oat milling business. He was industrious and thrifty and had contrived to save a very respectable sum. He had the traditional clan spirit and when a favorite nephew asked the miller to sign as surety, the request was not refused. At the time of the nephew's sudden death, the cashier of the bank, the funds, and the widow all disappeared—

they thought all together; but so much time had elapsed before the miller found out about it, they were not certain. However, none of them was ever found. This meant financial disaster for the miller and his family. As surety, he must make good the entire loss and that meant the immediate sacrifice of all he had managed to accumulate.

Sandy was then very young, but he retained a vivid memory of his mother's tears as, a little later, she saw the last of the choice family herd being driven away. Among the neighbors, little Sandy had a reputation for being precociously wise and clever with cattle and also for unusual industry and dependability. Besides, he was remarkably sturdy and active. Then, too, the entire family of the miller had the respect and sympathy of the farmers and townspeople about them. So it was easy for him to secure a position as chore-boy in the neighborhood when he was much younger than the other boys thus employed.

Another quality in the lad that endeared him to those neighbors for whom he worked was his unfailing cheerfulness. All agreed that little Sandy was as steady and faithful as a cart horse and as quick and active as a terrier. One outcome of the lad's good reputation was the gift to his mother of rather a substantial sum for the purpose of sending him to school. However, his mother decided that the money could be used to better advantage to purchase a coveted cow, which was to be the start of a new herd. Sandy was very proud of her determination to get ahead, and in after years stoutly defended her arbitrary action by saying that he considered he had done very well without such schooling. To this his wife would reply, "But what might you have done with it, Sandy?"

This often led to family arguments in which he

advanced the theory that all schoolteachers were lazy—rather an inconsistent attitude on the part of a man whose wife had been a teacher and in whom he had almost unbounded pride. Of her, the daughter Christina often said:

"In our home we never learned to use a dictionary because mother could spell and pronounce any word in question."

Later his mother modified her educational attitude, encouraging him to attend Bell's Veterinary School in Edinburgh. He would need this technical training if he were to become a master greve. She could teach him nearly everything else that he would need to know in this calling, she frankly admitted, but he could not get to the top without technical training as a veterinarian.

Hostility to formal education was by no means general in the Legge clan, however. For many years there has seldom been a time when a Legge has not held a professorship in one of the Aberdeen colleges.

While Sandy was working as a greve in the far northern part of Scotland, not far from Tomintoul, he met Christina Lumsden Fraser, "the bonnie school-teacher." This was in the general locality of Glenlivet. In this neighborhood is the picturesque Fraser home known as Upper Drum Inn. Here Christina Fraser was born and lived until she reached womanhood.

Christina was much more than "bonnie." She was profoundly conscientious and equally stubborn in her convictions. In her girlhood she came under the preaching of a Free Kirk minister who not only brought her to a conviction of sin but also impressed her so deeply with his dissenting doctrines that, rather than attend services in the comfortable Established Church near by, she more than once sat for two hours in Scottish rain and mist on the open hillside, with a little group of other dissenting enthusiasts and their leader.

By the time handsome and personable Sandy, the young farm manager, invaded her neighborhood, the Free Kirk people had a meeting-house of their own.

Although in his courtship of the popular "Kirstie" he met with lively and formidable competition, Sandy finally won the prize. They were married in 1852 and not long afterwards moved to Inverurie, and in 1853 Christina, named for her grandmother Fraser, was born.

Alexander the Miller had, after his staggering financial misfortune, contrived to make a fresh start and establish himself at New Mill, on Deeside, not far from Rob Roy's Bridge at Culter. Here they remained until 1857 and here a second daughter, Elizabeth, was born to the young couple. When this child was still a babe in arms, the young mother was swept by a tide of homesickness and a frantic desire to see her own mother again. This visit would involve a journey of not more than forty miles, but the primitive transportation available and the rough terrain made it a hard trip for a woman with two very young children.

As soon as this plan was known the older women of the Legge clan agreed that the journey was inadvisable, not to say foolhardy. Christina listened with white face and burning eyes and then quietly said that she must see her mother, that she was sorry not to take their advice, but she was going anyhow.

Her decision was a fateful one, for on the return journey the babe Elizabeth was taken ill and lived only a short time. The mothers of the Legge clan, whose advice she had disregarded, were not unsympathetic, but Christina felt the weight of their silent disapproval. The situation became unbearable and she confided to her husband that she could not longer endure the atmosphere of New Mill, heavy with blame for the tragic result of her wayward course. Two of her sisters had gone to America. Why not follow and join the elder of them, Mrs. McIlldowie, in Wisconsin?

This suggestion fell upon fertile ground, for Sandy was not altogether happy at New Mill. He was out of his element in the mill and restless to be again following his own calling. America, the land of unbounded opportunity—that was the place for him! With his knowledge of stock, his collateral profession of veterinarian, his strong body and his boundless energy, why should he hesitate to accept this challenge to splendid adventure and fortune? True, he did not know much about the progress that the McIlldowies had been able to make. Letters had been infrequent and mainly concerned with matters in which women were especially interested.

However, America was America; and the capital of 300 English pounds that he had been able to save ought to go far in a pioneer country where everything excepting money was cheap. Then there was Kirstie and her brooding unhappiness in the critical atmosphere of New Mill and Inverurie. She was eager for the big adventure.

Once he had decided to strike out across the Atlantic, he was in a hurry to be off. "Take as little as possible wi' ye. It'll be just as well to buy in America, an' far less bother," he counseled his wife. He even persuaded her to part with the gold-banded china which her mother had given her as a wedding present. There were tears in her eyes as she reluctantly yielded to this request. She mourned this sacrifice all her life, for nothing really fine in china was ever hers again, and her daughter Christina, who had gazed rapturously at these exquisite examples of English ceramic art when the table was set with them on rare state occasions, was sensitively aware of her mother's regret concerning them.

Pioneer Days of the Legge Family
in Wisconsin, 1857–1866

AFTER a dreary voyage in a little sailing vessel, they arrived in Canada and made their way to Sarnia, where Christina was overjoyed to be again with her younger sister, Mrs. Murray. The persistent illness of his wife in the Murray home after their long sea trip, depressed the active and vigorous Sandy and made him impatient to be making a start in "the States." Finally he proposed going in advance to Wisconsin and making things ready for his little family, his wife to follow as soon as she was sufficiently recovered. She readily agreed to this plan and bravely assured him they would soon be together again, starting their new home in Wisconsin. What a comfort it was to think that they would have the advantage of beginning with the snug little capital he had saved in Scotland!

He went with Mr. Murray to a Sarnia bank and secured United States paper money for his English funds and then crossed over to Port Huron, on the American side, to arrange passage on a lake boat to Milwaukee. With his fortune in bills of large denomination securely

ALEX LEGGE'S MOTHER IN HER LATER YEARS

stowed away under his rough working clothes, he had the comfortable feeling of being a capitalist in disguise. No one would suspect him of carrying a fat purse. Except for anxiety because his wife looked so wan and frail, he faced the future with a light heart and high determination.

Being hungry, he went into an inn and placed on the counter the one bill he had withheld from his money belt. Shortly the proprietor appeared. The bill was in his hand and a glint of trouble in his eye. Where had his customer obtained this bank note? It was counterfeit, worthless! Sandy's explanation convinced the innkeeper of his honesty. He then produced his other bills. They were all counterfeit!

In Scotland Sandy had never seen a bank note that was not genuine. He had heard of counterfeit money, but had never expected to own any. The innkeeper cautioned him that passing or attempting to pass counterfeit money was a serious crime and that the best thing he could do was to take the bad money back to where he had received it and attempt to recover on it.

Angry, humiliated, bewildered, he struggled with the problem of his next step. Should he tell his sick wife the terrible truth that they were penniless, that he had lost all of their little fortune, that he, the shrewd and competent Sandy, had been fleeced before he had set foot upon the soil of the States? There must be some way out of his shameful dilemma if only he had a chance to "think it oot."

Pondering, he wandered to the dock where a steamer was loading. An unmistakable Scot was superintending the task of getting a Clydesdale stallion on board the vessel and the powerful and frightened animal was putting up a spirited fight. Here was a situation that, for the moment, made Sandy forget his troubles. In broad Scotch he quietly remarked to the owner of the stallion:

"I'm Sandy Legge, an' if ye'll trust him to me, I'll get him aboard the ship without ony trouble. Man, but he's a gran' Clydesdale. This excitement isna' doin' him ony good, Mr. ——?"

"Galbraith, Janesville, Wisconsin," came the quick answer. "Well, try your hand wi' him, Mr. Legge. Ye canna do worse wi' him than these men are doin'."

Sandy took a few minutes to soothe the frightened stallion and then easily accomplished his safe loading by a method of his own. The Clydesdale importer then drew from his fellow-Scot the story of his experiences and offered him passage to Chicago, the destination of the animal, his expenses and transportation up to Janesville, Wisconsin, and "a wee bit more."

By the time Sandy reached the McIlldowie home in Scotch Settlement, located between Verona and Paoli, about fifteen miles southwest of Madison, he had, in a measure, "thocht his way oot" of his trouble. He would send the counterfeit money back to Murray and ask him to take steps to recover on it. The answer from his brother-in-law, a few weeks later, was reassuring. The bank would undertake to replace the spurious notes with honest money, but the transaction would take considerable time, as much red tape was involved. This response not only saved Sandy's face but restored his courage. He could work with a will so long as he could look forward to the ultimate return of the nest egg he had brought with him from Scotland.

Then he found his Kirstie with her sister, Mrs. McIlldowie, much improved in health and strength. She had come by the mail coach from Milwaukee, with the big "kist" containing all the household goods she had brought riding atop the lurching stage. Sandy's smile was back on his lips again and his eyes had their old-time twinkle as he played with little Tena, gave his wife a humorous account of his experiences, and planned with her the next steps to be taken in their great adventure.

They would have to remain for a time with the McIlldowies. Meantime he would look about for a farm that could be had at a low rental and would serve as a basis for his veterinary work and for dealing in horses. There was money in horses in this pioneer country for a man who knew them and could take care of himself in a trade!

The first thing to be done, however, was to pay for their keep for a little while at the McIlldowies. He knew their hospitality was warm and generous, but it went against the grain with proud and independent Sandy to ride a free horse to death. There was plowing and other work to be done on the McIlldowie farm and he was eager to carry his end of the load.

This brother-in-law stood well in Scotch Settlement and his word to neighbors and friends that the newcomer was a master veterinarian quickly brought calls for his professional services. With the McIlldowies, Kirstie and little Tena, he attended the Scotch Presbyterian church and made friends with the men of the congregation. Outside the church he was more given to talking about horses and cattle than to pious comment upon the sermon. This worldly trend of his talk did not, however, offend his new acquaintances standing about on the green of the church yard. They were quite willing to learn what they could about live stock from this authority, even on the Sabbath.

The turning of his first furrow in United States soil by Sandy Legge, in 1858, was in a manner which vividly dramatized the character and circumstances of this emigrant from Scotland.

His plow was pulled by a pair of young cattle in a gear cobbled from parts of discarded horse harnesses. So grotesque a substitute for the conventional ox yoke had not then appeared in pioneer Wisconsin, although it was common in the South and on the main trails to the Far West. But it aptly symbolized both the Scottish grit and the resourcefulness of this new settler in a primitive land.

He had secured the young steers in exchange for veterinary services but he was unable to get an ox yoke at once by this means and he had no money to buy one. Although clever with tools, he realized that making a yoke was a long and laborious task with which he was unfamiliar. So he quickly improvised a makeshift gear of leather that enabled him to start plowing promptly. The ready resourcefulness of Sandy greatly impressed Mr. McIlldowie. Here was a man who could meet emergencies by original, short-cut methods and make his wits serve him for money!

Shortly after the outbreak of the Civil War, Sandy decided that it was high time to strike out for himself and make an independent start, although the restitution money had not yet come from Canada. Fees for professional services as a veterinarian were seldom paid in cash and when he removed his family to a little log cabin on the "Black Farm," a few miles from Mt. Vernon, he found himself absolutely destitute of money.

Little Christina was the homesick member of the Legge family in the stark and crowded discomfort of the small log cabin. She spent many pensive hours recalling the homelike and substantial comforts of the stone house at New Mill with its spacious "but and ben" or kitchen-dining room and living room. It seemed to this child that

ALEX LEGGE'S FATHER, 1868

she had lived an enchanted life of comfort and elegance "back home" in Scotland. How long ago all this seemed —as remote as another existence! She silently recounted these memories, but talked little to her mother about them, for when she mentioned them her mother cried.

By his veterinary work and by shrewd trading, Sandy had contrived to accumulate a considerable assortment of livestock, including a number of gangling and raw-boned colts in which he could see great promise. But he had not a dollar to buy tea, sugar and other necessaries from the store. The Legges were very poor, even for pioneers of that day and place. Farmer Davidson, a young Scot of about his own age, advanced him a little money for groceries and allowed him to work it out quarrying stone and hauling it to where Davidson had a small part in the construction of the Federal military road then building through that section. The stones had to be broken with a sledge into small fragments. Sandy and his fellow-Scot put in long days at this heavy work, and lightened it by discussing the possibilities of wheat growing in Wisconsin and the opportunity of making money in the sale of horses for army use. What could he not do in the horse market with his $1500 nest egg, if only he had it!

The extremity of Sandy's situation in his first year on the John Black farm is illustrated by the fact that three or four calves were suckled on one cow and these nurslings were given a supplementary diet of tea made by boiling timothy hay mixed with a little milk. Every possible expedient to carry his livestock through the winter was resorted to and some of the more established and prosperous farmers contributed straw for roughage. Ultimately Sandy repaid them in neighborly services.

Across the road from the little log cabin was a double log structure in which Sandy established the first veterinary hospital in that region. It became a center of community interest and advertised its owner's profession to his great advantage. The door was fitted with a crude locking device and with huge wooden hinges which were never oiled. Their screeching when the door was being opened was ear-splitting. This was Sandy's ingenious protection against stealthy raids by horse thieves.

One odd circumstance contributed much to the popularity of the hospital. There were many Germans and Norwegians in this section of Dane County who had never owned horses until they settled in Wisconsin. To be the owner of a good horse filled any one of these thrifty and hard-working immigrants with an immense pride. Consequently, it was a common practice for them to overfeed their horses until they refused to eat. They were sick and must have the best veterinary attention obtainable!

This meant that they were taken to Sandy's hospital for treatment. After a serious examination of each of these animals, he would say that he knew "what's wrong wi' the beast" and that he could restore its appetite and strength in a fortnight or two. To his wife he confessed that his prescription was "just a wee puckle hay."

Another cause which contributed greatly to the growth of his veterinary practice was the prevalence of pneumonia among horses passing through the towns of that part of Dane County. In fact Sandy became quite a famous specialist in the treatment of this disorder. He well understood the reason for the common prevalence of this ailment. The freighters and drivers were often hard drinkers. Their overheated horses would be left without blankets at the hitching racks in front of saloons while their drivers went inside. Stops of this character were repeated in one town after another and the saloon-keepers generally advised the drivers of "shaking" horses, "Send for Sandy Legge, quick."

In case of a sudden storm or violent drop of temperature, Sandy generally went to Belleville or Paoli so that he would be instantly available. When he felt certain that a stricken horse could be saved, he had a horse of his own ready to trade so that the driver might continue his trip.

There is no denying the fact that Sandy acquired the reputation of being a sharp horse trader. However, he had his own peculiar horse trading code which he once carefully explained to his family. Miss Ina Sharman, his granddaughter, remembers this statement, a classic in the art of horse trading:

"I dinna cheat, but I ken a beastie better than most o' them. As they cam' doon the road I kenned what was the matter wi' them before I was near. That's my advantage. If a man wanted a trade, I told him all the weak points of my beastie right awa'. Being sure I hadna' told the worst faults, he looked for them and paid no attention to what I told him."

While living on the John Black place, Sandy received the refund on the counterfeit money, obtained through the good offices of John Murray. This enabled him to buy the Harker farm, a short distance away, and to enlarge his operations as a dealer in horses. Then, too, his collection of young stock of every description had matured and greatly increased in value. The war demand for horses was strong. Here was his opportunity and he had the capital with which to profit by it.

The large lumber operators in the near-by pine woods

to the north took much pride in their four-horse and six-horse matched teams and Sandy was an adept in catering to this demand. This was his "fancy" market—and a very profitable one. These were show teams. He fed them with grain from his own fields and they were fat and sleek. But he did not neglect other and larger markets for horses for the army, for street cars, for stages, for freighting, and for farms. The completion, in 1864, of the Madison-Beloit branch of the Chicago & Northwestern line through Oregon, Wisconsin, gave him a convenient shipping point for carload lots of horses.

Sandy worked at anything he could find to do, but his veterinary practice increased rapidly and soon took him over a wide range of country. This involved long trips, late hours, and family anxiety. Little Tena formed the habit of putting her ear to the ground so that she could hear the hoofbeats of his horse from a long way off.

One night as she listened, the hoofbeats stopped suddenly and she faintly heard a frightened call. She was not mistaken. A broken plank in a bridge had thrown horse and rider into the creek bed with the knees of the horse upon her father. He managed to work himself loose so that the animal got up without stepping on him and dashed on home, giving Tena and her mother a sickening fright. He was disabled for some time, but accepted his accident as an incident of rough pioneering life.

One day during Sandy's illness, Mrs. Legge looked out of the cabin window and saw neighbor men armed with cradles approaching the field of ripened grain. They had come to harvest Sandy's wheat for him as an act of neighborly kindness. But it was Sunday and Mrs. Legge was a strict Sabbatarian. She could not compromise with her conscience, so she went out to them and bravely explained her dilemma. Their kindness was appreciated, but she could not feel right to have the grain harvested on the Sabbath. They left good-naturedly, but were back in the field again early Monday morning. This woman who unfailingly appeared in their homes on occasions of illness and trouble could not offend them.

Sandy often chuckled at this incident and remarked: "Probably they went hame an' cut their ain corn that verra Sunday." He was at least certain that they did not hold him responsible for the incident.

Sandy's struggles on the Black place had given him habits of austere frugality and tremendous industry. After his little fortune was in his hands, he worked harder than ever and did not permit his thrift to flag. Living and land prices were up and therefore his nest egg did not count for as much as when he first arrived in Wisconsin.

Sandy became almost as ardent an enthusiast for wheat farming as livestock raising. In 1858, when he arrived in Wisconsin, wheat was bringing from 64 cents to 90 cents. At every opportunity he talked wheat with the older farmers who told him that the Crimean War had sent Wisconsin wheat prices from 31 cents to $1.70 in the period from May, 1854 to May, 1855. What are now the great wheat states were then only at the threshold of their development and Wisconsin considered itself an important wheat state, being led only by Illinois. Certainly wheat was the most important Wisconsin crop. A European war had increased the price of wheat at Milwaukee 448 per cent; if war should occur between the southern and the northern states, wheat prices would again soar. Sandy went in strong for wheat. In 1863 wheat brought

95 cents and in 1864, $1.30. Then came a drop in 1865 to $1.09, with a startling recovery in 1866 to $1.43 and in 1867 to $1.89.

The Army of the Confederacy was not the only foe of the northern states in the war years. The chinch bug invasion of Wisconsin began in 1860 and swept northward unresisted, almost unnoticed, for a considerable time.

Meantime there had been a tremendous influx of population into the western prairie states owing to the building of railroads and the opening of cheap lands to homesteaders and other settlers. These lands were ideal for the production of wheat upon a large scale and at greatly reduced cost. They were flat, fertile, and thus far unassailed by the armies of the chinch bug. The improvement of harvesting machinery exercised an enormous influence in this shift of wheat production to the great prairie states beyond the Mississippi: first the self-rake reaper, then the wire-binder which could harvest twelve to fourteen acres a day with two men on the ground to shock the sheaves. The great advance was the twine binder which came into general use in the early eighties.

Sandy watched the earlier developments of this wheat drama with the keenest interest and never lost an opportunity to talk with Mr. M. E. Fuller, of Fuller & Johnson, manufacturers of farm machinery at Madison. This acquaintance gained him the confidence of Mr. Fuller and ultimately had a most important effect upon his life and fortunes.

In 1866, having an opportunity to sell the Harker farm to good advantage, he bought in Montrose, just across the Primrose Township line. His standing rule in business was, "If you're offered what a thing is worth, take it; ye'll ha' bad luck if ye don't." The new farm, known as the Byam or Duppler place, was largely rich bottom land along the Sugar River. Sandy was forging ahead.

In the winter of 1861 Mrs. Legge was very ill with pneumonia and always thereafter was frail. This semi-invalidism prevailed throughout the period of their hardest struggle in the Mt. Vernon neighborhood, the log house era of their pioneering.

Sandy met this domestic emergency by "hirin' a girl," Mary Shepherd, daughter of their nearest neighbor. This domestic liberality was almost unprecedented and was commonly accepted as a striking proof of Sandy's affection for his wife. That Sandy, although high tempered, was unfailingly kind and considerate to his family is the testimony of Mary Shepherd Caldwell, at this writing ninety years old and living in Belleville, Wisconsin.

"Of course we all worked hard, but everybody did in those days," says Mrs. Caldwell. "I was called at three in the morning in summer and generally worked until nine at night and would then knit on the family socks. I'll never forget how proud I was when Mr. Legge voluntarily raised my wages to two dollars a week. No other hired girl anywhere about us got as much as that.

"Mrs. Legge was a gentlewoman who showed her good birth and training under all circumstances. They were superior people and this was evident in their family life. It was impossible to live in their home and not realize that Mr. Legge had great respect and affection for his wife. When I first worked there, out near the Devil's Chimney, times were terribly hard with them, but he saw to it that Mrs. Legge was spared hard household work in every possible way.

"Mrs. Legge had a black silk dress, so stiff and heavy that it would almost stand alone. Sandy, too, had fine clothes, a dress suit of finest materials. I never saw him wear it but once, and I shall never forget that time. One Sunday when Mrs. Legge was looking very sad and had not smiled for a long time, Mr. Legge disappeared and shortly returned, dressed in his fine party clothes. Then he capered before her until suddenly she broke out in a hearty laugh at this droll performance in a little log house."

III

"Little Sandy's" Birth and Early Boyhood,
1866–1876

IN July, 1862, Mrs. Legge bore a son who was named
George for his Uncle McIlldowie. He was frail and
nervous and had pneumonia every winter for the
first seven years of his life.

Four years later, in 1866, just after they had moved
from Primrose Township into Montrose, following the
purchase of the Byam or Duppler farm, she looked into
the eyes of another baby boy who appeared to be an
example of almost physical perfection. He was big, ro-
bust, and so happily disposed toward his surroundings
that he smiled serenely on the world about him and slept
soundly in spite of noise and confusion. He was promptly
named Alexander.

How many Legges have carried the name of Alexander
is a problem for the most patient of genealogists. The
name has persisted through at least seven generations and
probably more, to the confusion of even members of the
family. This resulted in coupling the calling of the particular Alexander referred to with his Christian name.
Alexander the Miller, for example, was the grandfather

of Alex. The substitution of "Sandy" did not help much, for each of the Alexanders was "Sandy" to his familiars, at least in youth.

On the maternal side of the Alex Legge line an equally confusing repetition prevailed. The number of Christinas back of Mrs. Christina Fraser, grandmother of Alex, is not on record, but it is wholly unlikely that the passion for this name originated with her mother. However, it is certain that this lady—and "lady" she was!—had four daughters, Isabella, Elizabeth, Christina and Jane, each of whom had a daughter named Christina. In the family annals they are designated as "Isabella's Christina," "Elizabeth's Christina," "Christina's Christina," and "Jane's Christina." The pattern was discontinued when "Christina's Christina," Alex Legge's older sister, decided that this family habit had gone far enough and named her daughter "Ina." Bright, sparkling Christina Legge would do that, for she had a mind of her own and a dislike of monotony.

From the day of his birth, January 13, 1866, Alexander was a remarkably self-sufficient and comfortable child. He was, to his mother at least, a symbol of the favor of Heaven. He reflected not one of her fears or frailties and all of her fondest hopes. God had answered her prayers for a man child made after the pattern of the sturdy Alexander Legges of his line—big, strong, unafraid.

By 1869 Sandy had achieved a moderate prosperity. He felt that it was time to acquire a home much better than any that had sheltered them in Wisconsin—one in which they would probably spend the remainder of their days and rear their children. His Scotch standards of substantiality could be satisfied with nothing short of a stone house, with a good farm as its background. The

Robert Oliver place met every requirement—160 acres of excellent land with a stone house that might have fitted into a Scottish landscape. This place was bought in March, 1869, and the following November a third son, James, was welcomed into the Legge family. Sandy had various other holdings and equities scattered about the county and was generally regarded as a man of substance.

When preparing to leave the Duppler place where Alex was born, Sandy thought it an opportune time to visit his people in Scotland. So, renting a comfortable house in Belleville for the winter, he put his family in it and started out for Scotland. At the Murrays, in Canada, he became rather seriously ill and was unable to get about until after the ship he planned to take had sailed. His illness left him weakened and depressed and he decided to abandon the trip to Scotland and return to Belleville. This was a bitter disappointment to him— until he eventually learned that the ship on which he was to have crossed was lost in a storm with every person aboard. When informed of the catastrophe, he accepted this deliverance as a sign that he should not return to Scotland. He never again attempted to do so.

The Legge home was in a state of high excitement the morning of April 11, 1871, which marked the opening of the spring term in Montrose District No. 6. Little Sandy had arrived at the age of five and was going to school along with "the big boys." As he trudged away to school, his mother habitually consigned him to the care of brother George—who often complained later that the hardest part of his guardianship was in fighting battles with the older boys resulting from Little Sandy's independence, stubbornness and spirit of mischief. This youngest of the Alexanders did not easily submit to the dictates of the leaders on the school playground.

In the five years in which Little Sandy attended this school he answered "present" at morning roll call 254 days. Very young children seldom attended winter school. Fighting their way through the deep snows was considered too great a hardship for them. Little Sandy progressed well in school, but liked better to work about the home as soon as he was old enough for chores of the lighter sort. His acceptance of responsibility was precocious and eager and he took great pride in "helping with the work"—filling the woodbox, feeding the chickens, gathering the eggs, and, at the age of eight, herding the cattle on a pony.

The great festive event of the year for the children was the opening of the apple trenches or pits. In the fall these were dug, thickly lined with straw, and filled with the latest winter apples. A heavy covering of straw and soil completed their protection from frost. Usually these nests of apples were opened about May 1, long after the stores of cellar apples had been exhausted. The fragrance and mellowness of these buried apples, as the pits were opened, sent the children into transports of joy. The opening of the Legge apple trenches was a community event, for this farm had been planted by Robert Oliver with the choicest varieties of winter apples in the entire countryside.

In his later years, Alex Legge was greatly intrigued by the story of the planting of this orchard. On the theory that the trees would thrive better and bear more heavily if they could be forced to send out a wide-spreading network of lateral roots, Mr. Oliver had placed a large flat stone below each tree when it was planted. Whether because of the stones or for some other reason, the trees had an amazing vigor and health, and their crops became famous throughout the entire region. When the apple pits were opened, the Legge boys took generous offerings of the choicest specimens to their teacher and to their schoolmates. And Old Sandy found a keen delight in calling in the children of the neighbors and filling their baskets with this buried treasure.

Regardless of how rough and fearsome Old Sandy was considered by those adults of the community with whom he had disagreements, the children looked upon him as their especial friend.

Apparently their welfare was a first consideration with him, for he had always kept a "wunter coo." In pioneer days cows freshened in the spring and went dry in the fall. The result was to deprive rural children of a supply of fresh milk in the winter months. Sandy Legge, however, considered this deprivation almost inhuman, so far as the children and invalids of his neighborhood were concerned. Consequently he never failed to provide a "wunter coo" and he was never happier than when filling the pails brought by children when milk was unobtainable elsewhere. This was his favorite philanthropy and the milk was free to all the children who came for it.

The first years in the stone house were happy ones. The farm yielded good crops and Old Sandy continued to prosper. And Little Sandy loved the new home, not so remote as the Duppler place from neighbors and their flocks of children.

Here gay, competent, enthusiastic, lovely Tena was married January 6, 1870. She was "half child, half maid," being midway in her sixteenth year. The bridegroom, Isaac Sharman, has always laughingly insisted that Little

Sandy stood up with him as best man. He clung stoutly and solemnly to Isaac's left leg throughout the ceremony. He liked Isaac, but was angry with him when he took Tena away to the Richard Sharman home across the fields.

A somewhat intellectual atmosphere prevailed in the Legge home. Old Sandy believed that "story reading" prevented the cultivation of a retentive memory and fiction was outlawed from the home. He even denied himself the weekly paper because it contained stories. Novels of Scott and the poems of Bobby Burns and Lord Byron contained, in his opinion, all the romantic reading that his children needed.

However, they had resources in this field of which he was uninformed. One of their neighbors was a Mr. Riley, an Irish gentleman who had been disinherited; but his brothers and sisters retained their regard for him and sent him books and magazines. Tena had the run of them and they included Harper's Magazine and Godey's Lady's Book. She obtained much of her education in the library of this eccentric exile.

The road home from school led past the Jimtown "Trading Post" which still bears that name. Alongside it was the blacksmith shop and here Little Sandy always stopped to examine the farm implements which had been brought there for repair. If the boys were late getting home from school, the invariable explanation was that Sandy had had to look at a machine in the blacksmith shop.

The devastation of the fine wheat crops in 1874 and 1875 was a hard blow to Old Sandy, for he felt that it spelled Wisconsin's permanent defeat as a wheat growing state. But a still harder blow soon followed.

Sandy Legge had many staunch friends among the Scotchmen of Dane County, but few of them were closer to him than a merchant named Findlay, of Madison. They frequently had business together and on several occasions Sandy had endorsed his notes. This fact was well known to a nephew of the merchant who worked in the bank with which they both did business. A sudden and extreme emergency arose in the banking affairs of Mr. Findlay which required immediate endorsement of one of his notes. There was no time to locate Mr. Legge. Not realizing the seriousness of his act, the young nephew signed Sandy Legge's name to the note, telling himself that he would explain to Mr. Findlay's frequent endorser what he had done and that it would be all right.

But before this could be done, the bank crashed and swept the merchant into bankruptcy. The young man in the bank made no attempt to conceal his transgression of the law. The amount to which the signature held Sandy was considerable—about $8000. This was sufficient to absorb his equity in virtually all of his holdings. To all practical purposes he was wiped out and was once more a poor man. This, following the disastrous chinch bug invasion, prepared him to accept the offer from his friend Fuller of an operating partnership in a 2000-acre ranch in Colfax County, Nebraska.

In narrating this incident to the writer, Miss Ina Sharman said:

"This happened a long time ago, but I think I have it straight, for I have heard it repeatedly referred to by Grandfather himself and by my mother. My father's recollection also confirms this version of the incident. Grandfather could have avoided all responsibility simply by denying that his signature was authorized. This he refused to do because it would have sent the young man to prison for a technical forgery by which he had nothing to gain. I often heard him say, 'I couldna' sleep o' nichts had I sent that young man to prison.' I think it one of the finest things my grandfather ever did. It reveals his sense of justice in a peculiar way. He was given considerable time in which to liquidate this obligation and made his last payments on it when he was in Nebraska."

The migration of the Legge clan from the densely wooded hills of Dane County, Wisconsin, to the fertile and almost timberless prairies of Eastern Nebraska was made in a spirit of high and exultant adventure on the part of the male members of the family, in spite of the disasters to Sandy's crops and finances. His thrift, industry, resourcefulness and business vision had brought him the friendship and backing of a man of wealth and enterprise who offered him a partnership in the operation of a ranch which seemed almost an empire to the emigrant from a crowded Scotch shire.

This elation over the impending westward advance was by no means shared by his wife, for whom it involved separation from her only living daughter, a sister, and many friends to whom she was much attached. Pioneer life promotes close and enduring friendships. A woman of warm sympathies, unusual friendliness and strong social instincts, she had attracted to herself a circle of devoted intimates. They lamented the thought that she was to leave them and perhaps she still more regretted that she must move on to another frontier.

This opportunity to better their fortunes had come in a year when severe and untimely frosts had destroyed the corn crop of their locality. Many of their neighbors killed their young pigs because they could see no chance of

BIRTHPLACE OF ALEX LEGGE,
MONTROSE TOWNSHIP, DANE COUNTY, WISCONSIN

raising them. Again, the wheat crop had been a steadily diminishing support so far as profit was concerned. The country was still suffering the effects of the historic depression of 1873—the most severe it had known.

This was no time for her to permit her personal feelings, however strong, to withhold complete allegiance to her husband's fortunes. It was the hour of his great opportunity as well as his great necessity, and she took her place loyally by his side and faced westward with a smile.

Although "Young Sandy" was then only ten years of age, he thrilled to the possibilities of this new pioneering adventure with singularly mature reactions. He plied his father with questions which revealed this precocious viewpoint. How many cattle would there be on this great ranch of Mr. Fuller's? How long would it take to break the thousand acres that were going to be put under cultivation? What would be his part in the work out there? His eyes lighted with enthusiasm when he was told that there would be hundreds of cattle on the ranch and scores of horses and mules; that he would be the head chore-boy; and that he would have a horse to ride and would be depended upon to "keep an eye on things" and learn all about handling cattle.

The picture which Young Sandy got in these talks with his father was that he was headed for a land where things were done in a big way, on a scale surpassing anything he had seen in Wisconsin, and that he was to have a personal part in this great enterprise. In the days immediately preceding their departure for Nebraska this serious boy seemed suddenly to grow up almost magically. His interest was in the farm operations which he would see and in which he would have at least a boy's part. The picture of a thousand-acre stretch of virgin prairie being attacked by a score of breaking plows impressed him tremendously. And cattle by the hundreds—he could scarcely wait to see this great new country!

Mrs. Legge told her husband: "No more horse trading when we get to Nebraska, Sandy."

Ranch Life in Nebraska, 1876–1887

TRANSPLANTING persons to new surroundings often works a magic as stimulating as is seen in the sudden development of trees and plants removed to new soil, kinder climate and freer rootage. Both Old Sandy and Young Sandy reacted sensitively to their removal to a new frontier of wider horizons.

The father clearly realized that under the new conditions he was going to find scope for the development of the business talent of which he had always been conscious, even in the darkest day of pioneering in Wisconsin. Now he had plenty of land and ample capital, for his wealthy friend Fuller had faith in his character, his industry, his business judgment and his remarkable knowledge of cattle, horses and crops.

Young Sandy seemed to have left his childhood—perhaps even his boyhood—behind him when his feet touched Nebraska soil and he saw the sea of virgin prairie billowing away to the southward from the ridge upon which the ranch buildings stood. Although only ten years old, he felt at the moment that manhood was almost upon him.

This sense of impending maturity gave him the greatest thrill he had ever known.

While the realization of this dream was not immediate, the vision was prophetic. He was soon to be swept forward in a personal development which was amazingly precocious. Every latent talent in the mind of this serious youngster was awakened into almost startling activity by his new surroundings and circumstances. He was to be his father's helper in a new business enterprise, in a new country and upon a grand scale!

The journey from Wisconsin to Colfax County, Nebraska, was made early in March, 1876. From the moment the Legges arrived at the Fuller Ranch, every day was crowded with activity and excitement. The plans for the development of the enterprise seemed vast to Young Sandy—almost beyond the grasp of his imagination. They were, in fact, on a scale unprecedented in that region. The family found temporary shelter in a little ramshackle house on the place. It was uncomfortable and inadequate, but a new and commodious ranch house was soon to be built upon a spot commanding a view of all the tillage acres of the place, the barns and feeding pens and a considerable stretch of the grazing grounds.

Then there were two and one-half miles of substantial and sightly fence to be built so as to inclose the ranch entirely and permit grazing on its pasture lands. An elaborate water system for the barns and feeding pens was to be constructed. This was to be supplied by a large windmill pumping from a deep well into a storage reservoir on the hill back of the barns.

The foundations of Young Sandy's education in the business of agriculture were laid in the family councils in which all projects for the development and operation of the ranch were discussed in detail. These were strange sessions, for the chairman of the Board of Strategy usually reclined in his bed. The physical relaxation afforded by this posture seemed to liberate his mental faculties. He seldom spent an evening sitting in a chair, but talked from his bed with his family. Even in working hours when some emergency arose, he would dash for his bed, telling his wife, "Dinna let them at me, Kirstie, till I can get things strechten'd oot in my mind."

Always Mrs. Legge and Young Sandy participated in these deliberations and George often shared them. The discussions generally focused upon the advisability of certain ranch improvements, but they also involved management plans that looked far into the future. Young Sandy was encouraged to ask questions and to speak his mind as freely as if he were an equal partner in the enterprise and his suggestions and objections were received in all seriousness. Not infrequently they were sustained and adopted.

Here was a striking example of family unity and carefully developed individualism that explains many things in the career of Alex Legge as an industrial leader and an agricultural statesman. In particular it explains his intimate and practical knowledge of farm problems.

These bedside deliberations were the high spots of his early years in Nebraska. No matter with what boyish abandon he might enter into the pranks of his young companions, he was a man playing a man's part, at sessions of the bedside Board of Strategy. It required remarkable mental nimbleness to keep pace with the reclining chairman in the calculations to which the soundness of proposed lines of action was subjected, but this tall, gangling lad demonstrated his quickness in mental arithmetic and seldom failed of a correct computation.

Still more important is the fact that his reasoning was remarkably clear and sensible. A statesman and economist of international stature once remarked to the writer: "The precision and clarity with which Alex Legge swept aside nonessentials and penetrated to the heart of an economic problem was a reasoning process, not an intuitive one; his conclusions were based upon a sound consideration of the essential facts involved in the problem, and did not result from super-hunches. He could trace clearly every step by which he arrived at a decision."

This commentator, however, did not know of the peculiar training that Alex Legge had received in dealing with difficult problems of practical agriculture in the family forum in which the development and operations of the Fuller Ranch were determined. Here it was that Alex Legge acquired the profound attachment for American agriculture that became the dominant interest of his life; here he sent down a tap-root into the soil that not even his extensive digressions into other fields were able to dislodge. He was deeply farm-minded to the end of his days.

Mrs. Legge greatly lamented the fact that this son was having so little schooling and, like his father, was being educated mainly along the lines of cattle-raising and agriculture. So, although Old Sandy ridiculed the need of schooling for such a big lad, the mother contrived to make it possible for Young Sandy and his brother James to attend an informal night-school, conducted by Charlie Wertz about the family table. Many extra sessions also were held in the haymow of the barn Sundays and on rainy days when there were brief interludes of leisure. An exposed strip of sheathing underlying the shingles served as a blackboard on which were chalked algebraic problems—particularly puzzles in mensuration which intrigued Young Sandy.

The most impressive sight to Young Sandy was the attack upon the wild land by the army of breaking plows which started immediately upon the arrival of the family. There were no stumps to dodge or dig out, as in Wisconsin, but the toughness of the mat of grass roots, undisturbed for centuries, was almost unbelievable. Soon there was a battery of more than a score of heavy breaking plows, each drawn by three or four horses or mules, attacking this virgin prairie sod. In later years, Alex often referred to this as one of the greatest sights he ever saw. Looking across the prairies he saw crawling ox teams doing the same work at what seemed a snail's pace by comparison. Each breaking outfit of three or four horses turned about two acres a day. In the hot midsummer, breaking began about two or three o'clock in the morning and continued until ten in the forenoon, to be resumed for a time in the cool of the evening. Meantime men and teams rested.

What amazed Young Sandy was the realization that this war upon the primeval sod was not a one-season campaign; that the first plowing had to be "back-set" or cross-plowed at a slightly greater depth and the sod given a chance to rot even before being sown to flax. Pulverizing implements were not then available. Young Sandy was filled with pride because their operations were upon a scale unapproached by any of their neighbors. No fall wheat was raised at that time; following the flax, the land was sown to spring wheat and oats. The sod was still too tough for the cultivation of corn. Charles Wertz, from the start a member of the ranch force, says:

"This period of breaking up the land covered four or five years. The wheat yield on the Fuller Ranch was twenty-five to thirty bushels to the acre. This gave a yield of from 15,000 to 20,000 bushels in a year in which wheat brought as high as $1.50 a bushel. They never had more than 800 acres in one crop. Their land was finally quite well rotated with corn and wheat. The Fuller-Legge outfit never raised nearly enough corn to feed their own cattle and hogs; in fact, the ranch formed the main market in Colfax County for corn and oats."

Old Sandy did not merely superintend the work on the huge ranch; he did much hard labor himself. From 1881 to 1884, each year over 1500 acres of small grain were sown. There were then no drills or seeders. One man drove the team, and Old Sandy sat in the back of the wagon, sowing the oats and wheat from early morning until late at night. He had long arms and could sow a width of seven corn rows with a swing of his two hands.

The Legges had left behind them in Wisconsin the devastating chinch bugs, but Old Sandy was to discover that his first crop of small grains had new and equally destructive enemies. One morning, at the break of day, he suddenly realized that thousands of wild geese and ducks were settling upon the grain fields for a feast, having come from their resting grounds along the Platte River. These hungry invaders spread out upon a hundred or more acres. Never before had he seen so stupendous a flight of wild waterfowl.

Excitedly he called to Young Sandy and Charlie to mount horses, ride out and scare the "honkers and quackers" off the fields. The birds lifted in vast clouds as the boys dashed toward them, shouting and swinging their coats above their heads. This flight was something to be remembered. Young Sandy much preferred this feathered crop enemy to chinch bugs. Fighting them was far better sport. Every man and boy who could muster a shotgun or musket was welcomed to the Legge grain fields. But in spite of this bombardment the ducks and geese destroyed many acres of small grains on the ranch. In the fall there were prairie chickens in great abundance. No king could have feasted his guests upon a greater or more tempting variety of wild game than appeared upon the Legge table day after day.

Eventually the wild geese and ducks became more cautious. Then the boys trained a "stalking cow" to permit them to shoot over its back. This was then a common practice; nearly every large ranch had one or more of these "hunting cows."

Young Sandy one day discovered that not even his pet hunting cow was exempt from his father's business rule that everything on the place was for sale at a price. It had been sold at a handsome premium, and when he complained he was told: "Train anither. It's good business, lad!"

Soon Young Sandy discovered that being chore-boy on a ranch of this size was a man's job in hard physical work and responsibilities. But he was strong and responsible beyond his years. His working partner on the ranch was Charlie Wertz. They became devoted and inseparable friends and Mrs. Legge encouraged this association. Charlie was steady, a little older than Young Sandy, and had a better education than most of the young men of that community. She saw to it that he was a member of her household, even when he taught the neighborhood school.

The ranch had hundreds of cattle in its feed pens and pasture lots, hundreds of acres under cultivation, and scores of farm implements. The machinery interested Young Sandy more than the livestock. He spent every spare moment studying it. As it came into use later, he demonstrated an almost uncanny understanding of its mechanism. If there was trouble with any machine, he was summoned. By virtue of his natural mechanical gifts he became the official repair man of the ranch.

Machinery on the ranch was furnished by Mr. Fuller who was engaged in the manufacture of farm implements back in Madison, and became agent in Nebraska for the Wood line of harvesters.

The first severe test of Young Sandy's stamina as chore-boy came with the calving season following his arrival. So many calves were born on the ranch within a short period that, along with others, he had to work all night. He was well schooled by his father in these veterinary duties; he knew what to do in emergency cases and acted with energy and dispatch. To lose a calf or a cow in the maternity ward of the Fuller Ranch was a rare experience under the Legge régime.

It was a great day on the ranch when the first importation of Aberdeen Angus cattle arrived. In Old Sandy's opinion they were the finest beef cattle in the world and he had great expectations of crossing them upon the Short Horns, the prevailing breed of his neighborhood. He did succeed in building up probably the finest herd of purebred Angus cattle in the United States and became widely regarded as the foremost authority in the country on this breed. The cattle operations of the ranch are described by Charlie Wertz in these words:

"In three years Old Sandy developed a herd of about seventy-five head of fine pedigreed animals. His library contained the most complete Polled Angus herd books in the United States. Also he raised many crossbreeds for feeding, besides selling breeding stock. The ranch pastured more than 600 cattle and fattened 1500 to 2000 head a year in the feed lots. Feeding operations were carried on twelve months in the year. This young stock came from the ranges in western and northern Nebraska, Colorado and Wyoming. They were fed until three and four years old and shipped to Chicago. In those days baby beef was unknown. Many mature fat cattle were sold for export—English 'Christmas beef.' They were fed from nine to twelve months and each consumed in that time from 100 to 150 bushels of corn. Frequently they weighed from 1500 to 1800 pounds.

"Feeding operations were carried on under a strict accounting system devised by Old Sandy. The books would show every morning the cost of a certain yard of cattle on that morning, including purchase cost, feed, labor cost, and cost from loss or death.

"Old Sandy was the only man I have ever known who could closely 'count' a herd of 400 to 500 head of cattle in two or three minutes. Out of a trainload of 400 he would rarely be off in his estimate as much as twenty-five head. First he would ride into the herd and get an idea of the size of the individual animals, then retreat to a considerable distance, scan them for an instant, and then call out how many he thought there were. The best explanation he could give of how he made his estimate was that he knew the space that a hundred such cattle should occupy when closely bunched—not, he confessed, a very convincing explanation. But somehow he got very close to the correct number. He bought on this judgment in blocks or herds. As I superintended loading the cattle, I knew the exact number of them."

Only as a free service to his neighbors did Mr. Legge practise his profession as a veterinarian after his arrival in Nebraska. Save in a single instance he obeyed his wife's injunction: "No more horse-trading." He traded a Percheron stallion for a quarter section of good land which adjoined the ranch. The huge creature was as fierce as a jungle lion. Before he would pass the animal into other hands, Old Sandy tamed him with a club. It was a battle that passed into local history.

As a judge at fairs and livestock expositions Old Sandy was in demand throughout the Middle West. This was regarded as real fame by the Scot who remembered with increasing gratitude the patience with which his cattle-minded mother had taught him the fine points of her favorite breed when he was a small boy. He was sensitively jealous of this reputation as an authority in the show ring.

On one occasion, for example, he awarded first prize in a class of young stock to a certain rather undeveloped animal over an older animal that had been fattened to the bursting point. The protest which followed this decision brought from Old Sandy the retort: "I'm judgin' breedin' cattle, not beef on the huif."

John Mitchell, a close friend of the senior Alexander Legge, says:

"Old Sandy was in high feather at a big cattle show. There was not a better judge of cattle in the whole state. His opinion was deferred to by the best breeders and judges in the West. On the judging bench he was in his element and let himself go for a good time. How he enjoyed it! But he did not need the atmosphere of the show ring to command the attention of any and all who knew him. On the street in Schuyler, Rogers or North Bend a group would instantly gather about him when he stopped to talk. His opinions on any subject were received with peculiar respect by his fellow-citizens. They all recognized the mental force of the man."

At one time Old Sandy sold a choice Angus heifer to a friend who entered it in the fair. Sandy had another heifer which he thought was even better than the one he had sold, but he did not enter it, choosing instead to enter an inferior animal so that his friend might win the prize. The judges gave this "scrub" heifer the prize because they knew it belonged to Old Sandy, the man who had promoted the fair.

He was furious, for he recognized the award as a piece of rank toadyism. At once he withdrew all the stock he had on exhibition. From that moment he lost interest in the local fair. This incident added immensely to his reputation for impartiality.

Old Sandy did not confine his importations to cattle; he sent to Scotland for men with training similar to his own. They were given $18 a month and board for their first year. His star "Scotties" were Walter Taylor, Jim and Pete McIntosh, Gordon Bowie, Robert Smith, Ellick Bayberry and William Rapler. About thirty others came to America on Old Sandy's invitation.

When the flax bloomed, it was generously sprinkled with yellow mustard. Old Sandy started a bunch of his "Scotties" pulling the mustard. From the upstairs window of the house he watched them with his field glasses.

They bunched close together, those in the semi-circle nearest the house occasionally pulling some mustard. But the group was loafing and almost stationary. Suddenly Old Sandy appeared on horseback. Quietly he assigned each man a strip about ten rods wide. This scattered them out, individualized responsibility and prevented visiting. Then he ordered, "Now pu' skellach!" None of them could understand how he knew what had been going on. In telling Charles Wertz about it later, he chuckled and said, "Chairlie, the verra next day they pu'd ten times as muckle skellach."

At fifteen years of age, Young Sandy was given responsibilities far beyond his years in the management of both men and livestock. When starting away for an absence of a day or two, his father would say to the men: "If onything oot o' the ordinar' turns up, ask Sandy. He'll ken." And Young Sandy had a knack in getting along with the help. They thought him a "rare lad." They liked him and took orders from him as his father's lieutenant without question. Thus, while in his early teens, he bought supplies and bought and sold cattle, hogs and horses at the ranch in the temporary absence of his father. This prepared him for buying on a larger scale. When it came to adding to the machinery equipment of the ranch, Young Sandy rather outranked his father. Machinery was considered his special department.

A tall milepost in Young Sandy's progress in his adolescent years was his first independent cattle-buying expedition. One day his father told him to go to a certain point in the southwestern corner of Nebraska, gather up a bunch of feeders which he had personally selected at an agreed price, and ship them to the ranch.

As the feeders were being loaded into cars at the nearest shipping station, two farmers from Iowa scrutinized them closely and asked, "Young feller, what'll you take for the lot?" Instantly Young Sandy added $1500 to the price which his father had agreed to pay for them.

"All right," was the prompt answer. "Come to the bank and get the money. That gives us a trainload of fine feeders without spending any time scouting about for them."

Young Sandy knew that this transaction was in strict accordance with his father's rule: "Tak' a profit when it's offered." Besides, he had looked about a bit and had located another lot of feeders which he regarded as a better buy than those he had just sold. He retraced his steps, bought the bunch which he had located and shipped them to the ranch, returning home with a bank draft in his pocket for $1500 net profit.

Old Sandy could not conceal his satisfaction with the transaction. Young Sandy was then about sixteen years old. Thereafter he was frequently sent out on buying trips with entire freedom to use his own judgment.

He was as strong physically as mentally. While in his teens he challenged any member of a visiting threshing gang to shoulder an open two-bushel sack of wheat with one hand without spilling any of the grain. Several attempted the feat, but failed. Then this boy gripped the edge of the open sack, stooped, "squirmed" his body under his right arm to give him a purchase and then lifted the sack from the floor to his shoulder. This feat gave him a greater local reputation than the fact that his judgment in farm matters was then as sound as that of an intelligent, experienced and fully matured man. Both his father and mother were intensely proud of the physical development of their tall son, born when his mother had feared that she would not be able to bring forth a child who would survive babyhood.

From the time of her arrival at the Fuller Ranch, Mrs. Legge was in frail health. Mr. Legge was prodigiously strong and it was difficult for him to appreciate the demands of physical work upon his wife's strength. He provided her with the best household help obtainable, but this was not always sufficient and she found it necessary at times to do more physical work than she should have done, or perhaps than she realized. Even the task of supervising the household activities of the Fuller Ranch home was heavy, for it was virtually a boarding house. Seldom were fewer than fourteen persons provided with bed and board within its hospitable walls and on frequent occasions that number was doubled. Friends and relatives from Wisconsin and elsewhere were invited to make long visits and Old Sandy made them doubly welcome because their presence brought smiles to the lips of his Kirstie. Many of the settlers about them fell into the way of referring to her as "Old Sandy's Lady." She commanded universal respect and affection throughout the region.

When he was about fifteen years old, Young Sandy, with his brother James, went to the near-by Brewery Hill School for two terms under Nate Woods, who later became a prominent educator. Later Sandy attended the Schuyler School for two winters. It was not then a standard high school, but carried excellent work about equal to the Sophomore class of today. There Young Sandy studied algebra, general history, advanced grammar and composition. He was a fine penman and a voracious reader, but his gift for mathematics was outstanding.

The task of furnishing the driving power for this ranch-

THE THREE LEGGE BOYS, 1879
JAMES, GEORGE, AND ALEX (AT RIGHT)

ing enterprise had become extremely heavy and at increasingly frequent intervals Old Sandy longed to escape from it. It was telling on his health and he became subject to alarming "dizzy spells." Again, certain irritations in his relationship with Mr. Fuller had arisen. Altogether, he decided that it was time for him to have a place of his own where he could work out his plans and theories independently and develop a home for his declining years.

For some time he had looked about the country for a place that would suit him and had decided that the Bollong farm, in the Maple Creek Valley five miles north of Rogers, met his needs. The soil was rich and the drainage good. Another important consideration was the fact that Neil Bollong was discontented and wished to get away. By some odd caprice of circumstances, this old sea captain had found himself stranded on the Nebraska prairie and had become homesick for salt water. He was eager to sell at a sacrifice, and Old Sandy, in May, 1884, bought this 240-acre farm and also leased a section of land one-half mile east. This was all raw land, good only for pasture and hay until it could be broken and cropped. Old Sandy started work immediately so that the buildings would be ready for occupancy when his contract with Mr. Fuller expired.

In connection with the building of this house, Mrs. Tom Thrush, of Schuyler, relates an incident which strikingly reveals the character of Old Sandy and his business dealings:

"My father's farm, known as the Plympton Place, had the only deposit of fine sand suitable for mason work in that locality. Father was interested in the upbuilding of the community and took the position that his contribution to community progress would be in the form of free building sand. When, in 1884, Old Sandy Legge started upon the building of a house of his own, he came to father for sand for the mason work and plastering. He was told to help himself. After he had secured all he needed, he asked the amount of his indebtedness and was told that it was nothing and that no man had ever paid father anything for sand.

"I was greatly impressed when Mr. Legge forced a ten-dollar bill into father's hand and declared with great positiveness: 'I will na' haul a pairt o' a man's farm awa' an' pay him naething for it.' He need not have paid a dollar for that sand—and ten dollars was quite a sum in those days."

The partnership with Mr. Fuller was dissolved, and Old Sandy's share of the cattle, after the market beef animals were sold, was more than four hundred head. These were sold to the V-R Ranch in Wyoming and were delivered by Young Sandy, his brother-in-law, Isaac Sharman, and Charlie Wertz.

Then the Legge family moved into the clean new buildings of their own Nebraska farm, which Old Sandy had determined should be called "Leggett's Den" and made as much like the ancient family seat of the Legges in Scotland as possible.

The progress of Young Sandy in the Schuyler School gave his mother high hopes that her big son was on the way to a college education. Probably there was not in the school at that time a student more intensely interested in his studies or one who ate up the more advanced studies, particularly mathematics and history, more avidly than Young Sandy.

But the historic blizzard of February, 1883, not only ended the mother's hopes for his continuing education but almost ended his life. On the day that the blizzard struck, Charlie Wertz volunteered to drive into Schuyler and bring Young Sandy home. The idea of allowing him to remain overnight in town was not entertained; any storm was a challenge to him and he might attempt to walk home. The fury of the blizzard had increased tremendously by the time they started home from the school. The cold was intense—more than thirty degrees below zero. They faced a driving snow so thick that they could scarcely see the horses. The only hope of keeping to the road lay in giving the horses a free rein and trusting their instincts to steer the course. When they reached home the young men were so far gone that they had to be lifted from the wagon and carried into the house.

In describing this experience, in later years, to Sam Faes and G. M. Durkee of the McCormick Company, Alex said that he knew he was as near dead as anyone could be and "stage a come-back"; that he would never again be afraid to die. It was easy!

With a characteristic grin, he added: "I guess the devil wasn't quite ready for me then or he would have kept me that time. The freezing wasn't so bad, but the thawing out certainly was hell!"

Out of this experience Young Sandy developed a pulmonary condition which greatly alarmed his family. This was the twist of fate that ended his formal education. About four years later, the family physician urged that he be sent to a dryer climate and a higher altitude. In delivering cattle, he had previously visited the big V-R Ranch in Wyoming, about 8000 feet above sea level. The activities of this ranch had fascinated him, and he looked forward to a life on the range with keen expectation. At his mother's request, it was agreed that Charlie Wertz should follow as soon as the school which he was teaching closed for the summer.

CHAPTER

V

"Big Sandy"—Wyoming Cowboy,
1887–1891

_____

T HE V-R Ranch was situated forty-five miles from
Douglas, Wyoming, then the terminus of the Chicago & North Western Railroad. It was stocked
with about twelve thousand cattle and with more than
fifteen hundred horses which were being raised for the
United States cavalry.

The two boys lived entirely in the open, day and night,
throughout the summer. They rated as "fence riders,"
receiving their keep and $35 a month.

Major Wolcott, manager and one of the owners of the
ranch, immediately recognized in Young Sandy and
Charlie Wertz young men of unusual intelligence, courage and dependability. They were promptly drafted for
especially dangerous service as payroll couriers.

The ranch was the supply station for a sawmill and
logging outfit, as well as for a tie-cutting company, and
the men all received their pay at the ranch. As checks
were not used, it was necessary to get from the bank in
Douglas large sums of cash to meet these payrolls. Each
week-end this ninety-mile trip was safely made, although

the territory was the stamping ground of scores of murderous outlaws. Sometimes as much as $5000 was carried back to the ranch at one time. Getting through safely was purely a triumph of wits. The couriers always started out on blind trails and never at the same time. The outlaws did not know which courier carried the money and could only vaguely guess the route each would take. On these trips Big Sandy—the name given him by the cowboys—took powerful field glasses. He knew when someone was approaching and changed his course accordingly.

Sandy's love for pranks was never outgrown. One morning the boys of the V-R Ranch learned that the Major had given orders for the cook to use up some old and wormy flour in making pancakes for breakfast. Big Sandy left the table without touching a mouthful. The others followed his lead.

When Major Wolcott opened his front door that morning, he saw a peculiar sight. There, staked out with their own ropes about their left ankles, were all the boys of the V-R Ranch, down on all fours and apparently busy eating grass—a pantomime group of silent Nebuchadnezzars.

"What the ——!" the astonished Major ejaculated. No answer.

Finally he exclaimed, "Go back to the chuck house and get your breakfast!" And they had a fine breakfast and no work that morning. The artistic success of this odd pantomime delighted Big Sandy. He had "got it across" to the Major without a spoken word.

The North Western was then being extended from Douglas to Casper. Perhaps Douglas was no worse than the typical rail-head town, but certainly it was wild and lawless enough to furnish material for the most lurid frontier literature, and it harbored a gang of horse thieves and desperadoes so powerful that they were in virtual control of the entire region and encountered little or no opposition.

On one of their rides, Big Sandy and Charlie came upon a covered wagon occupied by a young man, his wife and baby. They were fine, wholesome young people from the East and the V-R cowboys promptly made friends with them and took them under their protection. The team of horses owned by this young man was one of the best on the railroad grading job and the cowboys suspected that these fine animals would not long escape the eyes of the horse thieves.

One morning the horses were missing and news of their disappearance quickly reached the V-R Ranch. That evening Sandy and Charlie held a private interview with a man employed in hauling slabs from the sawmill. Their questions were interrupted by the grim warning: "You'd better mind your own business or you'll get your damned heads blown off."

To this the V-R riders replied: "Never mind about the other horses you have stolen for your gang. We've treated all that as your affair, not ours, and have said nothing. But this young man is our friend and if those horses are not returned to him within forty-eight hours, it will be your head that will be blown off. This is all we have to say. Now get those horses back to our young friend *pronto* or take the consequences!"

The steel grey eyes into which the slab-hauler looked gave authority to the threat. Next morning the horses were found grazing near the covered wagon. They were not again molested.

Visits at the camp-fire of this family were bright spots in the lives of the young cow punchers from Nebraska. These friends were like their own people.

In all probability Big Sandy would have been deeply involved in the warfare against the outlaws, horse thieves, and cattle rustlers that eventually marked the beginning of the reign of law in Central Wyoming, had he not received a letter from home saying that his mother was seriously ill and wanted to see him. He started at once on the home trail.

His ranching experiences were fascinating to him and he would gladly have continued them but for this call from his mother. Life on the range, however, had one drawback. Cow punching meant inhaling too much dust and this, he realized, tended to aggravate the trouble that had taken him to Wyoming. However, he left the big ranch with many regrets. He liked the cowboys with whom he was associated and regarded them as a "fine bunch." Then he recognized that there was adventure ahead in the inevitable conflict between the champions of law and order and the outlaws. This conflict was just about to break when he said his good-byes at the V-R.

To his delight, his mother's health greatly improved. Throughout her convalescence he spent much time with her. It was a period of rare companionship which he never forgot. That he had instantly returned home on learning of her illness was never for a moment regretted. His attentions to her were not only unfailing but almost pathetic. He provided her with every delicacy that he thought might tempt her. She could not express a desire that he was not alert to gratify.

Old Sandy told his son with considerable pride that he was now a County Commissioner, and Young Sandy soon found out that the entire countryside was being run pretty much in accordance with his father's wishes. Old Sandy seemed to dominate every group of which he was a member by sheer force of personality and ability.

That winter Young Sandy had another experience in a blizzard. One day early in January he and Charlie drove to Rogers, expecting to find Old Sandy. Instead they found a wire requesting them to call for him at Schuyler where he was attending a session of the County Commissioners.

Charlie Wertz gives this version of the trip:

"We left Rogers about two o'clock in a sleigh pulled by a span of big mules. Just west of the mouth of Shell Creek along the Platte, the blizzard struck us. It came on without warning—just one blinding mass of snow. The temperature was about thirty degrees below zero. When we reached Schuyler and found Old Sandy the town was as dark as at night. He insisted upon being taken home. This was wholly unnecessary, as we had left the livestock in the yard and there were two men looking after the farm. But Mr. Legge could not be dissuaded. I had just recovered from typhoid and Sandy insisted that I remain in town and avoid the exposure."

After driving for three miles, Sandy thought his father was freezing to death, so he turned in at the Hughes Farm. Driving in on the south side of a corn-crib, he tied the mules and carried his father into the house. Then he returned and put the mules in the barn. They stopped for the night in the Hughes home and left for Leggett's Den about nine the next morning. It took them until four in the afternoon to reach home, a distance of only a few miles.

The younger boys of the neighborhood were fond of

Young Sandy. He invariably had a quarter or a fifty-cent piece to add to their hoardings for a Fourth of July celebration or community picnic. John Paden, who then lived a mile from Leggett's Den, says: "When I was just a lad, I was taken very sick with diphtheria. Sandy came over nearly every night after the work was done, bringing me fruit and papers—luxuries on a Nebraska farm."

During this period Young Sandy stayed rather closely at home and indulged in much reading of a sort that he might have had in a preparatory school or college.

Occasionally there would be a dance in town. The Bohemian girls from the neighboring farms would walk to Schuyler barefoot, with their shoes hung around their necks. They would then put their shoes on and dance all evening. But when "Home Sweet Home" was finished, they were only too glad to take off the unaccustomed foot gear and cool their feet in the dew-drenched grass along the road back home. Sandy used to watch the young couples, but he never could be persuaded to join the dancers.

His favorite recreation was attending a literary club's meetings, where he took keen pleasure in discussion and debating. Fellow members say that Sandy always arrived at his point quickly and clearly, and that his arguments, while blunt and unadorned, were convincing.

The first power threshing machine in Colfax County was operated on the Legge farm and the future President of the International Harvester Company was directly responsible for the introduction of this startling innovation. Just where he first saw this machine is not entirely clear, but it is certain that he could not resist its appeal. Improved farm machinery was always alluring to him. The wheels of this thresher had broad rims, furnishing support to carry it over soft ground. Again, it would thresh many times as much grain in a day as the thresher operated by horses hitched to a long sweep.

Young Alex saw visions of making a light task of threshing the grain grown on the Legge fields and of earning good money by doing this work for the neighbors, many of whom were very extensive growers of small grains. He was so sure of the great advantages of this machine that the approval of Old Sandy was rather taken for granted. The machine would supply its own justification when he was given the opportunity to put it to the test on the home place.

One peculiarity of the machine was that it had no steering device but was guided by a heavy tongue securely anchored to the fuel wagon ahead, which, in turn, was hitched to the power engine. In his eagerness to make the start for home, Young Sandy started the engine moving before the tongue of the thresher had been fastened firmly. There was a sudden lurch and the tongue slipped out of place, injuring the hand of the man who was attempting to fasten it. It was a bad start, but the crew went ahead to the farm while the injured hand was being dressed by a physician.

Of course the accident had to be explained to Old Sandy who promptly declared that he would not have the "murderous contrivance" on the place. But Young Sandy was not to be denied without a struggle. In prevailing upon his father to witness one demonstration of the machine, he used the same patient diplomacy which was to be one of his best assets in the years to come. At last his father assented and the speed with which the machine devoured the bundles of wheat won the day for Young Sandy, who promptly organized a threshing crew of his own and moved from farm to farm in the Purple Cane community and then to more distant neighborhoods.

His mother was quite as anxious about his health as he was about hers, and persistently discussed with him his obligation to take better care of himself and to find some employment that would keep him out of doors but would not involve exposure to blizzards and to dust.

The first opening along this line that appealed to him was a temporary job assembling farm machinery for a local dealer. Here he was in his element.

As an incident of his practice of law, his brother George handled many collection cases for the McCormick Company's agency at Omaha. Young Sandy had greater success in pushing these collections than his brother; the result was that George advised him to go to Omaha and see if he could not get a job as collector.

He would have preferred to stay with the farm machinery dealer, but the position which he was advised to seek would have considerable to do with machines and it had the lure of more intimate contact with them in the future. Therefore he went to Omaha to ask for employment with the McCormick Harvesting Machine Company.

VI

Alexander Legge Begins His Business Career,
1891–1896

IN the spring of 1891, Big Sandy applied for a job to
P. M. Price, McCormick collection manager at
Omaha. He was then twenty-five years old. To the
question "Do you think you can collect tough accounts?"
he replied, "Yes; if they have anything to collect." This
shrewd answer gave him the job, on trial, at $50 a
month.

Undoubtedly his cowboy reputation was of substantial
value to him, for he was often referred to in company letters as "that young cowboy." Contrasted with the excitement of his Wyoming days as a courier carrying large
sums of money across a wild and lawless region infested
with murderous outlaws, his new job of collecting delinquent accounts from farmers looked like tame business to
young Alex Legge when he signed up.

The new job, however, had its advantages. It would
permit him to see much of his mother, whose failing
health gave him the conviction that she was not long for
this world. Then this new work would keep him out of
doors, which the family doctor told him was absolutely

necessary to his complete recovery from the pulmonary condition which had sent him to the higher altitude of Wyoming. Again, he liked the thought that he would be in a business connected with both machinery and farming.

Adventure, however, did not end for him with leaving lawless Wyoming. He had much to learn about the peculiarities of the farmers of the peaceful North Platte district. Those who had lately come from Central Europe had ideas of their rights as new citizens of free America which were fantastically confused. This he discovered in his first months as a collector—in the course of which he was often called upon to repossess farm implements on which collection seemed hopeless.

Farmers of this sort were often not only of highly explosive temperament but had the curious notion that possession and use of a farm implement made it theirs for keeps, regardless of the fact that it had come into their hands in exchange for notes on which they were supposed to make regular payments. Had those notes been United States currency instead of their own promises to pay, their sense of possession as to the farm implements delivered into their hands and baptized in their soil could scarcely have been more positive. The tools were theirs, and they would fight for them regardless of anything that anybody said about notes and past due payments.

This curious mental complex came to the young collection agent with dramatic force one day when, in a livery buggy, he drove into the farmyard of a customer from whom the company had been unable to secure any response by the usual preliminary communications. This was plainly a case for repossession.

The binder stood under an open shed. Young Legge

went directly to it and deftly extracted the knife. At that instant the farmer dashed out of the barn and rushed at the intruder, pitchfork in hand. Almost simultaneously an equally stalwart woman darted out of the farmhouse armed with a butcher knife. At once the tall young man with the binder knife began to whirl his ugly weapon in a wide circle, shouting to the driver of the livery rig to turn it, cramp the wheels, and be ready to give the horses the whip the instant Legge leaped to the seat.

The farm from which the collector had made such an inglorious retreat was owned by Banker Mickey of Osceola, Nebraska, later Governor of the state. Young Sandy drove at once to him, gave a humorous account of the experience, and remarked:

"I have a feeling that your fiery tenant doesn't like me. I'd prefer to deal direct with you. I'll forget the accrued interest for the company and the tenant's notes if you will give me your own notes for the price of the machine." This adjustment was readily accepted by the banker.

Alex Legge left behind him with the farmers to whom he paid his unwelcome visits an education in the fundamentals of business principles and practice of solid value. Had he been a missionary sent out for this purpose alone, he could not have done a better job in educating the immigrant settlers as to property rights and obligations. While he seemed to many of them a hard disciplinarian, he had a happy faculty of making them feel that he was really their friend, that they must respect the law and that it was their protection. His general attitude toward delinquent debtors from overseas who offered him violence was: "They don't understand. When they do they'll make good citizens."

This feature of Alex Legge's collection work is strongly

emphasized by both Sam Faes and G. M. Durkee who had charge of the Council Bluffs accounts throughout this period. Their testimony is:

"Alex made them come across, but he also made them realize the justice of his actions. He was patient and painstaking in explaining the whys and wherefores of every transaction. He was, in fact, a remarkable missionary of Americanization in the educational sense. Probably he did more than any other man on the prairies of Nebraska to teach the basic principles of ordinary business to the farmers of foreign birth. There are gray-haired men out there now—some of them holding public positions—who say of Alex Legge, 'He made me pay up, but he made me understand all about the deal, too.'"

There were others of established American lineage and thorough familiarity with our business usages who were more dangerous than the European delinquents. These men were the dregs of the homesteading era. They were not numerous, but their ideas of property rights were extreme—possession and use implied absolute ownership.

One of Alex Legge's earliest collection adventures was with a man of this type located near Greeley, Nebraska. Always Alex made his collection calls in company with a driver—in this instance his old friend Charlie Wertz. As they entered the premises of a man who had paid no attention to collection letters and had not made a payment on his note for several years, they found him leaning against his wagon box. He quietly asked, in good prairie English, the purpose of the call. As Alex Legge got out of the buggy and started toward the farmer, he began explaining that he came from the McCormick company to. . . . The explanation was not finished, for the next instant he was looking into the muzzle of a shotgun.

"Git into that buggy and pull out; the other feller is in already," ordered the farmer.

The young collector started to speak his piece again.

"Say, young feller," barked the defiant debtor, "ain't you got sense enough to know that I mean business? Now git goin' while the goin's good."

As they drove away, Alex Legge whimsically remarked to his companion, "I thought we'd eat dinner with that farmer. I'm mighty hungry—but I guess we'd better pass him up!"

The one thing that all such delinquents understood was that the implements they had bought were as essential to their farming operations as the soil itself. They were not to be dispossessed of these vital implements—not even if retention involved physical violence. Rural Nebraska had not yet outgrown the frontier viewpoint.

The delinquent accounts in the Alliance-Crawford territory were numerous and tough and Big Sandy was handed a thick sheaf of them, together with a generous allowance of expense money. In this first collecting expedition, he pitched the key that characterized all his later work for the company. He started out with the ingenuous idea that all he had to do was to present the company claims and the money would be handed out. Mr. Price knew that collectors frequently had been driven from farms at the point of a gun. This was to be the young collector's initiation and his superior expected that the tall cowboy would shortly return with few collections but with a rich fund of experience and disappointment. It was the hardest test that could be arranged for a greenhorn collector.

In about a week Mr. Price received a telegram from Big Sandy asking for more expense money. It was sent, but with instructions to come into the office as soon as it

STONE SCHOOLHOUSE AND CHURCH ON CROCKER HILL, WISCONSIN, BOTH ATTENDED BY LITTLE SANDY IN EARLY BOYHOOD

was nearly gone. Some ten days later Alex returned. His carefully prepared report showed that he had settled every claim given him for collection and had also sold twenty mowers to the agent at Crawford.

"Good Lord!" exclaimed his amazed chief. "When did you sleep?"

"I didn't, much," was the laconic answer. "I was afraid they might skip out on me before I got 'em."

As a consequence of this first collection expedition, Alex Legge was given a contract at $75 a month and expenses.

Under the law as it then existed in Nebraska, a note on which no payment had been made for five years became outlawed. Occasionally such notes fell into Alex Legge's hands, but he refused to consider them hopeless. The signers of these notes had been able for five years to evade making a payment. His practice was to appeal to a debtor of this class to make a small payment, no matter how trifling, as an "act of good faith." When this was refused, he made another type of appeal along this line:

"Well, the least you can do is to give me $2.00 to help cover the expense I have been to in coming out to see you."

Often this was successful and when a farmer responded by handing him $2.00, that amount was promptly endorsed on the note, with the result that the obligation was rescued from its outlawry. Sharp practice? Not as Legge saw it. The $2.00 belonged to the company and must be accounted for as a payment. Besides, in the Legge philosophy, any farmer who had had the use of a farm implement for five years without paying a dollar in return was not in a position to complain on ethical grounds regarding any treatment accorded him.

In the first period of Alex Legge's experience as a

McCormick collector his contacts were with retail dealers and their farmer customers. Joe Novak, a veteran implement dealer at Howells, Nebraska, illustrates the driving power of Big Sandy. They went together to the farm of a delinquent debtor. One glance about the premises convinced young Legge that his company would do well to recover the mower instead of trying to collect on the note. In an aside to Novak he said:

"Tell him I'm a machinery expert. Say nothing about my being a collector."

Of the farmer he asked, "Anything the matter with this mower?" This brought a deluge of complaints. After looking the machine over, the expert admitted, "Guess you're right. Tell you what I'll do. You take the note you owe, I'll take back the machine, and we'll call it square." To this the farmer assented.

The mower and the buggy were hitched together, tandem style, and the procession started back to town. It was a long, slow trip. They arrived late, but instantly Alex Legge began washing the mower and stopped for nothing until it was thoroughly cleaned. Then they had a belated supper.

"Now," remarked Legge, "the job is to think of a farmer you can sell this machine to right away—tomorrow. There's no time to waste." It was sold on the following day.

Mr. Novak declares this experience was thoroughly typical of Alex Legge in his early days as a collector; he was resourceful, put the business in hand ahead of his own physical comfort, and left nothing to be done later that could be disposed of on the instant.

G. M. Durkee, at this writing branch manager of the International Harvester Company at Omaha, was then cashier and bookkeeper of the collection department and was Alex Legge's inseparable companion. When the McCormick agency offices were moved across the river to Council Bluffs in 1892, they roomed together in the home of a widow and shared a double bed. Of this experience, Mr. Durkee relates:

"When I would come in late, Alex would either be folded up in zigzag fashion like an old-fashioned telephone bracket extension device, occupying three-fourths of the bed, or his feet would be stuck out over the footboard. He looked to be at least seven feet long!

"Those were days of happy companionship never to be forgotten. Alex was peculiarly a man's man—not interested in anything except his work. His concentration upon business was intense. There was no room in his thought for anything else. However, he did crave companionship and liked the atmosphere of a home. Eventually the widow surprised us by marrying, and this broke up our bachelor paradise.

"A little later I was married. By this time Sam Faes had come into the picture, bringing his wife to Council Bluffs. Alex persuaded them to give him a room in their house. This permitted him to continue much the same sort of life we had had together. He could talk business with Sam in the evenings as he had with me when we were living together. This kind of an arrangement suited him exactly. His consuming preoccupation with his work undoubtedly accounted in large measure for the amazing and almost austere cleanliness of his life. Temptations didn't bother him because his mind was so completely occupied with his work.

"I don't think I was more elated when the girl of my choice promised to marry me than Alex was when he was made collection manager about a year after he had entered the employ of the company on trial."

No collection experience of Alex Legge has been more often recounted than what is generally termed the "bull story." But the real point of this experience has been generally lost in the telling. A farmer in the wheat territory had bought a harvester and pledged as collateral a valuable bull. His payments on the obligation became sadly delinquent and all appeals to him were ignored. When Alex Legge called on him, the farmer announced that he was not in position to pay anything and that the company might as well forget the obligation, for the time being at least.

"Very well," replied the collector. "Where's the bull that you gave as collateral for this account?"

"Out there in that little pasture," answered the farmer, pointing to a piece of enclosed ground on which only a few chickens were visible.

"I don't see any bull there," said the collector.

"Of course you don't," laughed the farmer. "He's under the ground, not on top of it—dead as a mackerel."

"Get a couple of shovels," was the young collector's quick response. "His bones will bring a little something at the rendering plant." Alex Legge had no use for the bones of the dead bull but proof that the bull had been sold instead of buried would expose the farmer to prosecution.

The farmer was silent and thoughtful for several minutes and then said: "Hell! If you're that kind of a collector, I might as well pay up. If I do that, will you forget all about the bull?"

This was promptly agreed to and the account was settled in full.

Of all his collection experiences, none amused Alex Legge more than this:

In the case of delinquent customers who had drifted to unknown locations, it was the practice to send a questionnaire to the postmaster of the town to which, according to rumor, the delinquent had strayed. Such an inquiry was sent to the postmaster at Thedford, Nebraska, reading:

"Does Tom Ford receive mail at your office? If so, will you please give us the name of a collecting attorney or Justice of the Peace in your community?"

A prompt reply read:

"Yes; he gets mail here. Come on out and let's talk things over.

Thomas Ford
Postmaster & Justice of the Peace"

The invitation was accepted and the claim collected without any trouble.

The outstanding characteristic of Alex Legge's attitude as a collector was his alertness to help those against whom collections had to be pressed. It was his policy to nurse rather than distress a debtor. At Creighton he found an almost hopeless delinquent running a merry-go-round. Promptly he put an attachment on the outfit and placed a trustworthy young man in charge of its receipts. Incidentally, he gave the debtor good advice upon the proper operation of his business. When enough nickels had been collected to satisfy the claim, the outfit was released and turned back to its owner. This he considered a better course to pursue than taking over the show equipment and attempting to sell it, thus putting the man out of business.

Perhaps a more impressive illustration of this constructive policy is found in this incident:

Just about quitting time at the office, a telephone call from Fullerton, Nebraska, gave the information that the implement dealer there was on the verge of bankruptcy. Relations with him were purely on a commission basis and therefore the company's interest was solely in collecting the account. Alex secured a statement of the dealer's account and caught a train to Fullerton. Returning next day, he remarked:

"Well, I saved his business for him and at the same time secured collateral which fully protects us. The other creditors were just a little slow and I forced them to compromise with the dealer on a basis that will enable him to pay out in full; and he will keep right on doing business at the old stand. That's the sort of job I like to do."

"About Alex's only recreation," relates Mr. Faes, "was attendance at the services of the Unitarian Church. The old pastor talked more of human relations and morals than of formal religion. He was a philosopher and an intellectual.

"I do not recall that Alex ever went to a theatre, except sometimes to a variety show in the course of our annual dealers' convention when it was necessary to entertain customers. Occasionally we bowled on Saturday nights in the basement of the Kiel Hotel with the employees of our bank. Sometimes we would take a bicycle ride into the country for exercise.

"Whenever possible we would go to Rogers and spend Sunday at Leggett's Den. These were certainly strenuous vacations. We always did a hard day's work to 'earn our dinner.' I was glad to get back to the office and rest up. Alex's strength and energy were tremendous. Hard physical work was a relief to him. How he did enjoy these visits with the family—particularly with his mother! And he never failed to take home a load of table delicacies and other presents."

From the time that Alex Legge had an office desk, its pigeonholes began to accumulate the I.O.U.'s of friends and acquaintances. Many of these were not redeemed, but he still continued to accumulate them.

It was very difficult for Alex Legge to resist any appeal for help. The sorriest mendicant on the street could work him. Although he knew that the money would in most instances be spent for drink, he could not bear the thought of denying a meal to a hungry man. This led him to have printed a quantity of orders on a certain restaurant for twenty-five cent lunches. These he always carried in his pocket and handed one out to every pan-handler who appealed to him.

The big event of 1892 in the midwestern office of the McCormick Company, was the arrival from Chicago of the general manager, Mr. E. K. Butler, a very forceful man. He was dissatisfied with the general agent there and had plans by which to rescue the organization from its static condition. He had studied the reports of the "cowboy collector" and had formed the impression that he might prove to be quite important in rescuing this big agency from its deplorable state. Unofficial reports had drifted in to him that "the tall cowpuncher" was an eccentric individual, afraid of nothing, clear headed and a glutton for work. He might prove to be the key to the whole situation. He would at once get acquainted with him. Not so easy. Mr. Butler was a big, impressive, dignified man. At luncheon time he said:

"Mr. Legge, you are going to lunch with me."

"No," was the prompt and blunt answer. "That hotel is too swell for me. I'll stick to my 'Greasy Spoon' and see you afterwards." And so he did. Instead of being offended, the high company official recognized the independence and fearlessness of the tall cowpuncher. It pleased him and he placed immediate confidence in "Big Sandy."

The historic panic of 1893 gave the management of the McCormick Company no opportunity to deal with reforms in the branch office on the banks of the Missouri. These were allowed to drift until 1894 when Mr. Butler came on again and Sam Faes had joined the agency staff as bookkeeper and cashier, directly under the general agent. This placed him in a strategic position. The delicate task which Mr. Butler delegated to Mr. Faes was to keep on under the general agent but look to Alex Legge for leadership.

"If you need help," said the general manager, "signal for it and I'll back you. We can't let the business in this great territory die of dry rot, but there are diplomatic reasons why it is desirable to have the general agent quit on his own initiative."

"I was not then well acquainted with Alex Legge, as I had joined the office later than he did," Mr. Faes says. "At the start he gave me the impression that he had a very good opinion of himself, but I soon discovered that this was not egotism but simply an understanding of what was necessary to be done, and a knowledge of his ability to do it.

"His constructive foresight is illustrated by the stand which he took which brought the whole organization matter to a head with unexpected abruptness. As head of the collection department in the territory, Alex took the position that the logical way to improve collections was to improve the quality of the accounts delivered to the collection department by the sales department. The general agent could not see it this way. He wanted the work of his salesmen to be unhampered by considerations of the collectibility of the sales accounts. His policy was to make every possible sale and then dump the obligations thus created on the collection department; that would be Legge's worry.

"Here a brief glance ahead becomes necessary. This situation continued for some time until Alex Legge went to Chicago and had it out with Mr. Butler. The time had come for a show-down and he made this clear in no uncertain terms. Before he left, it was agreed that if we were not sustained in our position, we would immediately resign. In fact, we had picked our landing field with another Omaha implement company. Mr. Butler, however, refused to accept our resignations, gave Alex Legge a substantial raise in salary and promised us that the general agent would soon be out of the picture.

"Let me say here that meantime Alex and I had become intimate friends and at his request, when Mrs. Faes came on and we started housekeeping, he came to live with us.

"I suspect that Mr. Butler wrote him quite frequently and confidentially indicating a wish that he would keep an eye on affairs in the sales department, although that was technically not his responsibility. However, it was not so difficult for Alex to do this for the reason that his powers of leadership were so apparent that they just naturally compelled the respect of every man in the organization—with the possible exception of the general agent's."

Early Days in the McCormick Company's Service, 1893–1899

THE first years of Alex Legge's service as collection manager at the Council Bluffs agency could not have been timed for a harder test of his abilities, courage and endurance. In much of this unhappy period the forces of nature and economics seemed to have joined in a cruel conspiracy against the farmers of that great food-producing territory. In 1894, for example, only the creek beds of Central and Western Nebraska showed signs of growing vegetation. These were slender ribbons of green winding through vast stretches of barren desert. The usually productive areas did not yield enough to feed the settlers. And then came the scourge of grasshoppers.

The financial depression was prostrating to all business everywhere and its punishments fell with especial force upon those industries which depended most directly and intimately upon agriculture. The only bumper crop of this sad period was of political revolutionists. Alex Legge certainly had his work cut out for him in this era of drouth, grasshoppers, and political and economic chaos.

The cold of the winters was as extreme as the burning heat of the summers. While working for the company out in the cattle range country, Alex spent a memorable night in a country hotel at Arnold, Nebraska. He arrived in town after dark, and the hotel keeper was already in bed. Alex pounded and pounded at the door. Eventually the proprietor called from an upstairs window: "Come on in and find a bed for yourself. It's too cold for me to fuss around."

Alex went in and found himself a bed and crawled into it. But the bed was cold, for the only stove in the house excepting the kitchen range was in the office which served as a general lounging room. In spite of the fact that he was hardened to the rigors of the "wide open spaces" and had his overcoat and other clothing spread over the covers of his bed, he was chilled to the bone and could not sleep.

Finally he dressed and shiveringly descended to the office. There he put fresh fuel into the stove and then virtually embraced it, gratefully absorbing its heat. It was a record night for low temperature and piercing winds.

He was dozing in the early morning hours when the front door opened and admitted the local mail carrier whose abundant whiskers were festooned with icicles and snow. As Uncle Sam's hardy mail courier removed his cap, opened his outer garments and prepared to thaw out over the stove, the future president of the International Harvester Company glanced up at him and asked a single question:

"What room did *you* have?"

Some of Alex Legge's most thrilling experiences in the cattle and wheat country were in fighting his way through blizzards to shelter.

The deadlock between the general agent and Alex Legge was broken in the spring of 1896 by a message from the general manager to Alex Legge instructing him to rent a suitable house for the accommodation of young Harold F. McCormick and his bride who had returned from a long honeymoon tour. There was no concealment of the fact that Mr. McCormick was to succeed the undesirable general agent. Here was a move which could not be checkmated.

Alex Legge carried out to the letter Mr. Butler's instructions to completely refurnish the house. It was already equipped with fine old furniture, draperies and other accessories in exquisite taste and the owner wished to leave them for the use of the McCormicks. But Alex Legge had received his instructions and therefore these artistic pieces were promptly placed in storage to make way for others representing his idea of what was suitable for the daughter of John D. Rockefeller and the son of Cyrus Hall McCormick. There was no denying that these new pieces were substantial.

Alex Legge was almost nervously anxious to see how the McCormicks would react to the attempt of a "cowboy bachelor" to prepare an acceptable abode for them. He had never before selected furniture or furnishings for even a room for farm hands; but Mrs. McCormick's appreciative exclamations of delight, as she first viewed the rooms, completely silenced his misgivings.

She played her gracious and kindly rôle so well that on future visits in the home he did not notice the disappearance of one massive piece of furniture after the other or the replacement of the rugs and hangings he had bought at a local furniture store. No pains were too great to be taken to avoid wounding the feelings of this new friend to whom both the McCormicks quickly became attached. He liked them both and adopted them as his particular responsibility. But let Harold McCormick tell in his own way the beginnings of this rare friendship which never faded.

"From the start," says Mr. McCormick, "I frankly admit that, being totally without business experience, I felt rather timid and fearful in my new situation. I was only twenty-three years old. The attitude of the general agent whom I was to succeed was unfriendly and his personality repellent to me. Imagine, then, the relief I felt in realizing instantly that Alex Legge was my sincere friend and that I could rely upon him to see me over the rough spots in learning the business. He looked to me then a veritable tower of strength. He was all that, and more, as I was to learn by long experience. But it is a satisfaction to me that from the first time I saw him I realized his inherent power, his frank ingenuousness, his intuitive and sympathetic understanding of human nature and the soundness of his judgment.

"I knew at the outset that I must lean heavily upon him. Our relations might have been difficult and embarrassing but for his great common sense, his courage in brushing aside any thought that, because I was my father's son, he must deal gently with me and prevent me from learning by hard experiences the lessons I needed in order to become a useful and worthy member of the McCormick organization. Alex Legge could not have toadied to the King of Great Britain. It was not in him to do that. Yet he had a most delicate perception of all the proprieties in our relationship, even after I became general agent, thereby ranking him in the organization. He respected the rights of my position and at the same time maintained his own, never failing to place his amazing wisdom at my disposal when I had the discernment to ask for it.

"Probably his hardest task in teaching me the business was to force me, in a diplomatic way, to make my own decisions. Soon after my arrival he allowed me to gain a very salutary lesson at the expense of great discomfort to himself.

"We had been out together watching the work of a corn harvester in a field on the west bank of the Missouri, some miles south of Omaha. When the demonstration was over, I suggested that we cross the river by rowboat and return by the trolley line running to Lake Manawa. Immediately he assented. Later I realized that he must have chuckled inwardly at the nature study lesson I had before me. We had no difficulty in getting into the near-by boat, but when we were a considerable distance from what appeared to be solid ground on the opposite shore the boatman informed us that he was grounded in mud and we would have to wade ashore. Here was a new and dismaying form of athletics, but I had proposed the expedition and would be a poor sport if I backed out.

"Stepping out of the boat we found outselves knee-deep in clinging Missouri River mud. The bank to which we finally made our way was densely covered for some distance back with willows. I climbed one of the tallest of them for a view of the country beyond and to determine the right direction. Suddenly I found myself crashing down to earth from a considerable height. I landed on my side and left an imprint in the mud from which, after it hardened, a very clear cameo of my profile could have been cast. Alex was too kind to laugh or even grin.

"After floundering around for some time, we finally

found our way out of the bewildering forest of willows and reached the trolley line where we caught a car into Council Bluffs. There we went to the back door of my home by a route as secluded as possible. We were both extremely tired and hungry and as dinner was waiting, our preparations were decidedly casual. That must have been a most amusing dinner party for Mrs. McCormick. But she was entirely equal to it and laughed at our account of the adventure. Of course Alex Legge had known from the instant I proposed the trip by rowboat that I was in for a lesson in Missouri mud that I would never forget.

"Mrs. McCormick admired Alex Legge immensely. We both felt his intellectual force and were sensible of the privilege of an intimate association with a man of such mental stature. He was refreshingly simple and direct, and engagingly human, as great of heart as of mind. Utterly lacking in social polish and sophistication, he compelled recognition that he was a gentleman in the most vital definition of the term. His rough exterior covered a rich endowment of fine feeling and natural discrimination in his human relationships. Most often his roughness was displayed to conceal emotions of tenderness.

"In all the period of our association in Council Bluffs, both before and after I was made general agent, we did not have a single clash. Often I pressed my views in opposition to his because I wanted to get a real understanding of the problem in hand. Sometimes I followed this course deliberately as a means of drawing him out. Alex liked and encouraged this attitude.

"When finally I became general agent and his ranking official colleague I often had to make quick decisions on my own responsibility. But I'm glad to confess that always I had the reassuring feeling that Alex Legge would somehow prevent any grave error of judgment on my part from going through to the serious detriment of the business. Consciousness of the availability of his rescuing hand was a great comfort to me.

"Sometimes his opinion was a little difficult to secure because of his determination that I should make my own decisions. The development of my individual judgment was his constant objective and I owe him more than I can ever say. One result of our intimate association in the Council Bluffs office was a close friendship covering thirty-seven years. When I left Council Bluffs to take up new duties in the Chicago office, I had a feeling of sadness that our intimate daily association had reached at least a temporary end. At the railroad station when he bade Mrs. McCormick and myself good-bye I felt that he regretted the ending of this chapter of our friendship as sincerely as we did—this in spite of the fact that his promotion to the position of general agent was involved.

"I distinctly recall making, at that time and for my own benefit, a mental appraisal of Alex Legge's outstanding characteristics in the handling of business. Briefly, my summary was that he was always on top of his job, always ran his work and never permitted it to run him. In other words, he did not allow himself to become tangled in the smaller problems and details of the business at the expense of the larger ones. He kept a high and clear outlook unconfused with the lesser problems of the hour. He was a long-range thinker.

"Although he called his organization associates by their first names, he had an innate dignity which did not permit undue familiarity. In this particular his poise was remarkable. By the same token, he respected the dignity of his business associates. Back-slapping was not one of his accomplishments and I never knew anyone to treat him with that gesture of familiarity.

"One of the main elements in the confidence which Alex Legge inspired in those who had personal contact with him was the fact that his reasonings and his decisions were based upon practical experience and close personal observation. He was not a theorist. Experience had been practically his only school and his loyalty to his alma mater was unswerving. He was gifted with a combination of great determination and tenacity. This was not, to my mind, stubbornness, but something very much above it. He could and did yield to the opinions of others when convinced that he was in error and when this occurred—which was not often—his yielding was wholehearted and gracious. He was too big and too honest to stick stubbornly to an opinion when his good sense told him that he was mistaken.

"Perhaps some considered him a hard taskmaster but certainly he was unsparing in driving himself. His industry was the greatest of any man I have ever known. Work was more fun to him than play and therefore, in his maturer years, he did not know how to play, as that term is generally used. Perhaps one reason for this is that he had an iron constitution, great physical strength and resilience, and a consuming interest in the business of the company. Because the great burden of his work was mental, he welcomed every opportunity to use his tremendous physical powers. This was sometimes rather hard on those who tried to keep up with him in field demonstration work, for example. Again, he made nothing of physical hardships and exposure that most men could not endure, even those accustomed to outdoor life in the prairie country. He was no playmate for a man not seasoned to physical hardships."

There were no vacation entries in Alex Legge's personal calendar while he was located at Council Bluffs. With one exception, the only respites which he allowed himself from office work were week-end visits to the family home at Rogers. This exception was the entertainment of the Sharmans and his brother James at the World's Columbian Exposition in Chicago in the intervals of business conferences at the company's headquarters. In spite of the anxieties of the panic and the financial and industrial confusion which reigned throughout the country, he enjoyed this outing immensely, for he was very fond of his sister Christina, her husband and their daughter Ina, then a young girl. The unforgettable beauty of the White City and the appeal of its scientific and industrial exhibits afforded him less satisfaction than giving these members of his family a big time. He particularly enjoyed a closer acquaintance with the "little redhead" as he called his niece Ina. They became close comrades.

Throughout the last years of his mother's life, Alex wrote her several times a week, no matter how great the pressure of business or the inconvenience of writing. As a correspondent he was equally faithful to his sister, whom he always addressed as "Sis." Each week she received a letter from him—and generally from George and James also. Keeping in close touch with one another was a strong characteristic of the Legge family.

The week-end visits to Leggett's Den were not occasions of unalloyed happiness for Alex because of his mother's rapidly declining health.

On one of these visits he took Harold F. McCormick with him and suffered genuine embarrassment from the frankness of Old Sandy, who bluntly told the guest of honor: "Ye're spilin' a good farmer, takin' Sandy into that pothering business."

While Alex's salary was then only a little over $200 a month and his father was in secure and comfortable circumstances, he bestowed upon his mother every comfort and luxury he could find. A procession of baskets of fruit and tempting table delicacies was shipped to Leggett's Den. In these dark days Alex would ride long distances in order to spend the Sabbath with his mother.

The year 1894 was draped in black for Alex Legge because of his mother's steadily wasting strength. The abysmal business conditions which prevailed throughout the country and particularly in his own territory compelled him to do much traveling, but he made these trips as brief as possible. Mrs. Legge's Spartan attitude is indicated by what is perhaps the last letter he was to receive from her:

At Home
Friday afternoon

Dear Sandy:

We are still alive but the heat is intense here today. I think I have a touch of the grippe for I feel miserable. The boys are at the manure —say they are pretty well along. Cut corn last week, but this week have been fixing up for the tobacco.

Have had Will Pirie six days but he has rented eighty acres from Pa of the Jones land and commenced breaking today.

We have had twice a good shower but it soon disappears—the heat. Pa thinks the corn is not improving as there is so much of it not cared for. They are feeding the cattle great loads of it every day for two weeks. Think they will cut corn again next week. The hay is hardly worth cutting. If it would not be so hot!

Had a card from Tena a few days ago. They were well. Hope you are keeping better. Think it may be some cooler out there. Jim is to take this down this evening and see if there be any word from you. Hope you will soon be back.

God guard and guide you, is the prayer of your loving

Mother.

This last epistle to her son Sandy not only throws a clear light upon the relationship between them but it was a letter after his own heart for it dealt mainly with the material affairs of the family, with an irrepressible up-welling of maternal affection at its close. He could read between its lines a wealth of repressed emotion, of affection for him and sympathy with the sufferings of the people of the panic- and drouth-stricken region in which her lot had been cast. Their understanding, as mother and son, was most unusual. There were many things which they did not need to say in words. Mrs. Legge died on the 28th of August, 1894.

A few months later Mrs. Caldwell and her daughter came to Leggett's Den from Wisconsin to make a home for Old Sandy until the Sharmans could arrange to close their house in Evansville, Wisconsin, and come to Nebraska for a stay of indefinite duration. They arrived to make their home with the master of Leggett's Den in the spring of 1895. Christina Sharman had made many trips to Nebraska and, in view of her father's lonely situation, had decided to take up a permanent residence with him. He was very fond of Tena and her daughter Ina and greatly liked and respected his quiet, unobtrusive, substantial son-in-law. Bereavement, however, had not subdued his positive and forceful nature; his likes and dislikes were as strong as ever and as positively announced. He did not, for example, care for music; but Tena was an enthusiastic musician and her daughter Ina shared that talent and enthusiasm.

One day Mrs. Sharman suggested to her father that Ina's musical education was being interrupted and she would like to rent a cottage organ for his granddaughter's use. Old Sandy replied, "There'll be nae kist (chest) o' whussles in this hoose!"

One of the happiest events of Old Sandy's last years was "Jimmie's" marriage to Elizabeth Johnson, in April, 1897. This romance developed when all of his other children were absent from Leggett's Den. Thus he and his youngest son were alone in the desolated home save for the competent "kitchen help" he always supplied. The house seemed very empty to companionable Old Sandy, who was also in poor health and needed someone to look after him.

Suddenly this youngest of his boys began "going out" and giving careful attention to the span of blacks and the new buggy, and to pretty Elizabeth Johnson, who belonged to one of the finest families of the community. Old Sandy was far too canny to betray his satisfaction with this situation.

At the outset of his romance Jimmie conformed to prevailing rural practice in the methods of his courtship—waiting in line with the other young swains at the church door to greet the girl of his choice with: "May I see you home?" Three times in succession Elizabeth Johnson "handed Jimmie the mitten" by slipping past him in company with her mother. Then he decided that it was high time to use his head. He reasoned that Mrs. Johnson was different from the other mothers in the community, more conventional in her social standards. The next Sabbath evening he called early at the Johnson home. He was admitted to the house by Mrs. Johnson to whom he explained that he was calling on her to ask the privilege of taking her daughter to church. This request was promptly granted. He had demonstrated his social discretion and won the day.

Immediately upon his acceptance by Elizabeth, young James told his father that he would bring home a wife April 7; that they would be married privately at the par-

sonage, stop for a call upon Mrs. Johnson, and then drive
home. James had asked his bride not to change her wedding dress after the ceremony. When Old Sandy caught
his first sight of her, his eyes filled with tears, for the fab-
ric of Elizabeth's wedding dress was identical with that
which his own bride had worn. Christina Sharman, who
had arrived to welcome her sister-in-law, took a small
remnant of her mother's wedding dress from between the
leaves of the family Bible to prove that they were of the
same iridescent maroon silk.

Elizabeth fitted into the home. Old Sandy's approval
of her was unqualified. And when she gave birth to a
boy, he was named Alexander and became his grandfather's idol. When the child reached high-chair age, the
two "supped" together at an early tea and Old Sandy
taught the youngest Sandy to use the broadest of Scotch
dialect. Of course Little Sandy's first suit was of the
Gordon plaid. He had to be taken to the gallery in Schuyler and be photographed in it. Elizabeth was tactful and
yielding when any of Old Sandy's whims were encountered and he was happier in his last days than he had
dreamed he could be when his Kirstie faded from his
sight.

Old Sandy loved all children and would stop to talk
with any who did not run from him because of his huge
stature and loud voice. Occasionally he would return
from trips into town and gleefully relate that "the wee
trooties" had talked with him as if he were "nae a fearsome body."

Alex spent a certain Christmas at home while the "harvester war" was at its bitterest. He confided to his father:
"The Deering people have offered me more money than
the McCormicks are now paying me." Old Sandy

snapped, "Bide where ye are. Dinna ye ken that the McCormick's 'll fin' it oot if ye are worth more than ye are gettin'?"

Old Sandy enjoyed most of his visits to Wisconsin, particularly while his wife was living. He went back twice after her death, once in 1895 and again in 1899. On these occasions he stayed with his daughter Christina but spent the days in riding about the country and renewing his acquaintanceship with old neighbors.

In May, 1900, only a few months after he had been in Wisconsin, Christina learned by letter that her father's health was extremely poor. She went to Leggett's Den and urged him to return to Wisconsin with her. Old Sandy shook his massive head and said, "Tena, the doctors want to get me awa' from hame to dee on your hands. I'm goin' to dee aboot the first o' July."

In speaking of this, later, Christina remarked, "Father always had an uncanny way of being right. His prediction impressed me dreadfully. He died July 11th."

He was buried in the Purple Cane Cemetery where his wife had been laid to rest six years before. Shortly after her death he had sent to Aberdeen, Scotland, for a monument of granite, hewn by Scotch artisans. It now stands on the family burial lot.

George Legge, who had been his unfailing defender on the Montrose school grounds where the aggressiveness of "Little Sandy" was continually getting him into trouble with his playmates, held a peculiar place in the affections of his brother Alex. He envied George his scholarly ability. In fact, the entire Legge family was very proud of the learning of George and had no doubt that if distinction ever came to a son of Old Sandy, George would win it.

In the fall of 1885, George entered the University of

Wisconsin and completed a four-year course in three years. He had not long been practicing law in Omaha, however, when he had a severe breakdown, in 1904. Sometime later he moved to California where he and Alex had bought an orange ranch, and in this climate he recovered from his lung trouble. He engaged in the real estate business in San Diego until 1925, when he died of an attack of angina.

VIII

On the Highroad to Business Leadership, 1899

WHILE knocking about his territory in the late nineties, Alex Legge continually pondered his mother's urgent pleas that he should become "an educated man." These carried more weight with him than when she was living to reiterate them, for he now had a fuller appreciation of her wisdom than ever before. Therefore he determined to attend a state university and eventually prepare himself for the practice of law. His work brought him into constant association with lawyers and he felt there were great possibilities in this profession and that he would like it. Then he recognized that if he was ever to make this radical change in his life, it must be done immediately. A few more promotions in his work would make it impossible to change.

He regretted that he had not done this before when it would have been easier, but always there had been obstacles. One of the greatest of these was sickness in the family and the opportunity to help out with the financial burdens. Again and again he said: "It's all I can do and I want to do it." He felt, too, that going to college would involve scrapping all that he had achieved since he had entered the employ of the McCormick Company in 1891. For him to go to college would, he felt sure, seem strange to most of the men in the organization who had come to look up to him as a "go-getter" and a business leader. It was a case of now or never and he packed his trunk in preparation for resigning his position and starting for the state university.

At this crossroads a message from Harold F. McCormick forced the decision that took him up the highway of industry. The message was a summons to Chicago to take charge of the company's collection interests throughout the world. This change, made in 1899, was the turning point of Alex Legge's career. It imposed a severe test of his capacity suddenly to expand his horizon to world dimension, to broaden from provincial to cosmopolitan, to think and plan on an international scale.

He had never been outside the United States and scarcely had strayed off the prairies of the North Platte territory. All he knew about foreign countries he could summarize on one sheet of the company's letter paper in his fine flowing hand. And then, in the phrase of his cowboy friends, he wasn't even "city broke." They had their doubts that he ever could be, because he was at heart a social "rebel"—the term they applied to wild range horses that could not be broken.

Business considerations, however, were always foremost in his mind and there were plenty of these to think about. Complete reorganization of the collection system of the company throughout the world was his job. Then, too, a comprehensive reorganization of personnel was on foot. Mapping the lines of operation in the United States did not worry him. Out in the North Platte territory he had dealt with almost every type of American, native and alien. The foreign field, however, seemed set with pitfalls and problems utterly unfamiliar to him. The set-up had its peculiar variations in the different countries and these must be recognized and met or the business would suffer. In the main, relations abroad were with principals, large distributors, rather than with individual purchasers and users of the company's products and therefore the moral and financial responsibility of these distributors must be predetermined with especial care.

In the earliest company conferences which he attended he kept his feet firmly on the floor, sat stiffly erect with folded arms, said little save in response to questions personally addressed to him, and did not tell a story or indulge in a single cynical "wisecrack."

In this period of unnatural repression he worked as furiously in gaining a mastery of the essential facts of the foreign situation as if he were fighting his way through a Nebraska blizzard. A number of the foreign representatives of the company were at headquarters and he subjected them to a barrage of questions. Says one of them: "He didn't overlook a thing that was important for him to know."

Of course the new chief of the collection department was not expected or required to show his hand at once. He was given time to grow used to his new environment and to gather and assimilate the facts necessary to the careful preparation of collection plans covering the entire world. In this strenuous period he gave a brilliant demonstration of his characteristic ability to brush aside nonessentials and strike straight to the heart of a subject, emerging with a clear and definite course of action.

When finally he submitted his plan to his colleagues, it

received general commendation. Each of its provisions was of course subjected to challenge and debate. Then it was revealed that Alex Legge could talk. He explained every point in his plan with crystalline clearness. At the same time he revealed an attitude of open-minded receptivity to the ideas advanced by others, together with a fearlessness in defending a proposal when he was unconvinced that the criticisms of it were valid. The consensus of that conference was that the latest addition to the executive staff certainly was not a "yes man."

The acceptance of his plan did not, however, give the newcomer any feeling of triumph. His attitude was that he had done the job to the best of his ability and time alone would tell how many mistakes he had made. Meantime, his bodily relaxation and his occasional injection into the conversation of a homely anecdote or a sharp flash of wit revealed that he was becoming more at home at the council table which was destined never thereafter to be quite as formal and sedate as before his coming.

On arriving at headquarters in Chicago, following his novitiate in Council Bluffs, Harold F. McCormick had become first vice president of the McCormick Company. In this capacity he often presided at the council table because his elder brother Cyrus, then president, was frequently absent in New York, busy with the prolonged negotiations that eventually ended in the formation of the International Harvester Company.

Harold F. McCormick gave this picture of Alex Legge's rise to a place of leadership at that table where he was at first so repressed and uncomfortable:

"I recall with great distinctness how this newcomer from the North Platte country made his place with the strong men at the council table. He was very quiet in his first months there, but gradually he began breaking his restraint, asking sharp questions, flashing shrewd suggestions, and making brief comments that brought smiles to the lips of his colleagues. Immediately before and after the merger, changes in the personnel of the management were numerous. Following the merger, Alex Legge was made assistant manager of sales. But he did not remain long on this rung of the ladder, his next promotion being to the post of assistant general manager, under Clarence Funk.

"These two men presented a striking physical contrast, Funk being a small man and Legge very tall, his every movement suggesting physical strength. By this time Mr. Legge had begun to feel at home at the council table and to let himself go with something of the freedom with which he had conducted informal office meetings back in Council Bluffs. Loyalty and kindness were two of Alex Legge's strongest characteristics and they were subjected to a hard test in this period of adjustment while Funk was his ranking superior. I watched both of these top-notchers very closely and it was fascinating to see Mr. Legge's consistent and sometimes painful struggle to speak his mind and at the same time maintain due respect to his immediate superior.

"When the two men entered the council room, everyone there at once greeted the assistant general manager as 'Alex' and when he spoke in the discussions, his remarks commanded the closest attention. In a word, without meaning to do so, he 'stole the show.' Inevitably when Clarence Funk retired Alex Legge succeeded him as general manager.

"Legge was a born leader. His mind was always open to conviction and he considered all the facts and all the opinions of his colleagues. Then he struck straight from the shoulder, regardless of any opposition. He considered that he owed this blunt and courageous honesty to the company. Occasionally he held his own opinion in reserve until circumstances developed in a way to clearly support his conclusions. Then he would drive home his convictions with great positiveness. I recall one occasion when he took issue with a vice president and gave him a very hard riding. When it was over, that official grinned amiably and handed Mr. Legge a cigar with the remark, 'Have a cigar, Squire.'

"When I became president, in 1918, the by-laws were changed, eliminating the position of general manager. The new set-up was a group of vice presidents, each in charge of a distinct branch of the business, reporting direct to the president. Alex Legge was elected senior vice president, being in charge of the entire company under the president. When this change was made, he came to me and asked if his old title of general manager could not be hitched up to his new title. While he was proud to be vice president, he hated to give up the title which he had always liked and which had meant so much to him when he acquired it. He always clung to old and familiar things, and would not readily abandon an old hat or suit of clothes.

"In later years his attitude toward the Board of Directors was very interesting to observe. This attitude was most respectful, but it seemed to me that he usually expected that his opinion would be adopted. There were a few notable occasions when his advice was rejected by the board. It is only fair to say that, judged by subsequent events, it often turned out that he was right. His marvelous ability gave his associates a feeling of security in his leadership; there was the conviction that we were peculiarly privileged in having so great and wise a man to guide the company's destinies. This reliance upon him sometimes tended to dull the sense of individual responsibility in his administrative colleagues, and that was not his theory of how to run a great corporation; but he could hardly blame anyone for this attitude because his vision was so penetrating and constructive that dependence upon him seemed almost inevitable.

"One of his traits which I most admired was his capacity for growth. His training had been wholly in the school of experience and he never felt that he was graduated from it. His mind was intensely acquisitive and every departure from his routine had a broadening effect which was clearly apparent. His first trip to Europe was a case in point. But this result was most obvious when he returned from his service in Washington during the World War and, years later, at the end of his strenuous experience as chairman of the Farm Board. Had these experiences added inches to his physical height, his growth could not have been more apparent. His vision of life was immensely broadened by them.

"Many who did not know him intimately thought him wholly materialistic. From my intimate association with him I cannot accept this estimate; I feel that he was no more materialistic than Abraham Lincoln. He was Scotch and very practical and he could see through material problems with amazing penetration; but my conviction is that he had a spiritual vision that dominated his life. His interest in his fellow men was unabated to the day of his death. This was evident in the disposal of his property, in which he revealed a profound purpose to serve the interests of humanity in general, and particularly to promote the well-being of the farmers of America.

"Too great emphasis cannot be placed upon this cardinal trait. His humanness was catholic and comprehensive and took no account of social strata. All men came within the warm circle of his regard and concern. It was as easy and as natural for him to strike the hand of fellowship with a farm hand, a machinist in the shops, or a dock hand as with a great financier or diplomat.

"It is scarcely too much to say that he became acquainted with almost everyone in the organization. Of course this was not literally true, but it was true to a remarkable degree. On one occasion the desirability of having a certain minor executive get out on the territory came up in the council. To this he made the comment:

" 'I've dropped in on him occasionally and made that suggestion. His desk is stacked high with papers and his invariable excuse is that he must clean them up before he can get away. The last time he offered this alibi, I told him he reminded me of a rat milling around in a barrel of chaff. If he doesn't take that hint, I'll take his papers away from him.'

"Mr. Legge could not tolerate indecision or delay on the part of any subordinate in pushing through work that had been assigned to him. While he respected the feelings of those under him and gave them a chance to do any job allotted to them, he had no hesitation in relieving them of the assignment and doing it himself when they held up the traffic. This happened scores of times in the executive offices. Any man who fussed over details was an irritation to him. It was difficult for him to understand indecision on the part of an executive who had the facts before him.

"Some were inclined to regard him as a conservative,

ALEXANDER LEGGE AT ABOUT 22 YEARS OF AGE

but I cannot take this viewpoint. There were times when, with respect to expansion, for example, his boldness sent a tremor through his colleagues. On the other hand, there were also times when they were aghast at his conservatism. This is only another way of saying that, with his great vision, he saw far into the future and perceived business trends not discernible to most eyes. This he demonstrated in anticipating the slump of 1921 and taking steps in advance to meet the exigencies of that trying period. He performed the still more difficult task when the speculative crash of 1929 plunged us into the greatest depression our country has ever known.

"Alex Legge's administrative policy was peculiar, perhaps unique. He would not spend a dollar on a building designed to impress the public with the magnitude of the corporation. To his mind that sort of symbolism was a waste of good money. On the other hand, he would allot millions and perhaps tens of millions for expansion and engineering developments. No machinery that would cut the cost of production or improve the quality of the product was too expensive for him. There was, however, a catch in these provisions: they must be paid for out of earnings and not with borrowed money.

"The engineering department always found him ready to listen to any proposal for the development of improvements in machines already made by the company or of new machines to expand the company's service to the farmers. Thinking ahead was Alex Legge's long suit. His firm conviction was that the best way to hold the position of the company was to lead in new and improved types of machines. The lure of the experimental workshops was irresistible to him; and a field test of a new machine was certain to command his attendance.

"Improving the quality of the machines produced by the company was constantly in his thought. On one occasion, for example, he happened to spy in a dealer's junk pile a defective casting which he seized and carried back to headquarters. The foundry that had produced this part received from him a caustic calling-down which remains in shop tradition.

"He had a Scotch abhorrence of debt, personal or corporate. The Harvester Company has never had a funded debt and only once did it put out a note issue. There was no fat in this for the financiers and no one made any money on that issue. Mr. Legge was always insistent that a note of the Harvester Company should be as good as if it bore the imprint of the Government. This, of course, implied that the company must always keep itself in a financial condition to support its paper. Therefore he insisted upon regularly putting back into the business a part of the earnings. No financier was ever able to argue him into departing from this simple and conservative procedure. His response to such advances was that the Harvester Company would stick tight to the ground and make its progress on its own power."

CHAPTER

IX

The One Romance in Alex Legge's Life,
1908

THERE was only one romance in the life of Alex Legge—the romance that flowered into his marriage, in 1908, to Mrs. Katherine Hall. He was then forty-two years of age and his closest friends and associates had felt that he was likely to live out his days as a single man. This opinion was based on the fact that to a peculiar degree he was "woman shy." In adolescence and early manhood he did not display a sentimental interest in any of the girls of his acquaintance. He was friendly in a casual way but seemed remote, unreachable and unconscious of their charms. He simply was not interested in them because of his intense absorption in work and business.

This indifference persisted after he went to Council Bluffs and began work with the McCormick organization. There he frequently went out with the young men and girls of "Implement Row" for moonlight parties on Lake Manawa and enjoyed the gaiety and good fellowship of these occasions; but no young woman was able to interest him.

When Alex Legge first met the remarkable woman he was to marry years later, she was the wife of Tom Hall, a lawyer at Ord, Nebraska. This was shortly after Big Sandy became head of the McCormick collection department for the North Platte territory. Hall impressed him as a keen young lawyer, especially adapted to the legal end of collection work. Mrs. Hall helped her husband in the office, and it did not take Alex Legge long to observe that this young woman was an important member of the legal firm. He learned that she had taught school, had studied law while working as a stenographer in the office of Judge Coffin, of Omaha, husband of her older sister, and had been admitted to the bar.

Tom Hall was an engaging young man and the fact that he was a lawyer gave him a certain standing with her that her other suitors did not possess. She was devoted to him and felt that together they would achieve professional success. When Alex Legge took to their office the legal collection business for the territory around Ord, the Halls were greatly elated.

After Alex Legge was called to the Chicago office of the McCormick Company, the collection agency of the Halls was moved there. Naturally he saw much of this young couple, both at their office and in their home. To the last day of Tom Hall's life, Alex Legge continued to be his friend and helper. After Hall's death, reliance upon Katherine in the handling of the affairs of the collection agency brought the young widow into constant association with Mr. Legge, resulting in a fine friendship. They went about together socially and he brought her in contact with his sister and with his close friends and business associates.

While their marriage was not an elopement, it was

planned to be very private. Ina Sharman gives this account of her uncle's wedding:

"We had then left the old home farm at Belleville and were living at Evansville, Wisconsin, convenient to Madison. Katherine Hall came to our place after having been for some time in Pennsylvania on account of the illness and death of her father. About a week later, the day set for the wedding was at hand. The atmosphere was thick with secrecy. I think Uncle Alex gave out the idea that he was playing the game of putting one over on his friends and associates. This didn't fool any of us. We knew that he was suffering from an acute attack of shyness.

"Only the minister, Rev. T. W. North, and the Baker family from across the street were in the secret. Mrs. Mary Ann Crocker, my father's sister, had come to visit us for a few days without knowledge that a wedding was to take place in the family. It seemed very appropriate that the old Crocker neighborhood should be represented at Uncle Alex's wedding, even inadvertently.

"Shortly after the marriage, my mother discovered that Aunt Katherine had relieved her of the great responsibility of looking after Uncle Alex. From that moment she ceased to worry about him. In the years immediately preceding the marriage, my mother had become the very close friend of Aunt Katherine and I think she understood better than anyone else the diligent, tactful, and devoted care which Uncle Alex would receive from his wife. 'He is in good and competent hands,' she declared."

Thomas Coleman, of Madison, Wisconsin, was a pioneer farm implement man and his home was a favorite rendezvous for those connected with the Harvester Company. Here Alex Legge and Katherine Hall visited frequently after their marriage. Both Mrs. Coleman and her daughter, now Mrs. Leo Lunenschloss, became her devoted and intimate friends. Perhaps no other person is better qualified to draw a portrait of Katherine Legge than Mrs. Lunenschloss, who told the writer:

"I loved Mrs. Legge more than anyone I ever knew outside of my own family and I believe that my mother felt as I did toward her—and Mother was a keen judge of character.

"It was not altogether easy to become really acquainted with Mrs. Legge. To strangers she often appeared rather stiff and formal, very correct and perhaps a bit distant. This impression disappeared, however, when one really came to know her. Perhaps this impression was in a measure due to the way she had of sitting stiffly erect, not touching the back of her chair. Dignity and poise she always had. While she had great enthusiasm for everything she undertook, it was of a quiet sort. Her taste was exquisite and her competence was the envy of all her friends. I think of her as the finest homemaker I ever knew.

"The wife of Alexander Legge did not have an easy part to play as hostess in his home, for he was socially untractable and did many things which were rather unconventional. His wife became very adroit in covering such things or preventing them. The social education of Mr. Legge as a host was interesting to witness and I observed it with intense admiration for his wife's tact.

"Mrs. Legge had an irrepressible sense of humor. This was the Irish in her. I always think of her as laughing—never loudly, just a restrained chuckle. When she was greatly amused, tears would often stream down her cheeks. She had a fine natural complexion and mischievous grayish-blue eyes with dark lashes and eyebrows. Her black hair had a sprinkling of gray in it. She looked best in tailored suits with hats of the sailor type.

"Katherine Legge had a remarkably keen and clear mind, well ballasted with common sense. In many particulars her mentality resembled that of her husband; but she had the advantage of feminine intuition and natural social discrimination. All of her mental and social gifts were completely devoted to promoting her husband's interests and to making him comfortable and happy. She had no social ambitions for herself. She was intensely human and warm hearted. It is no wonder that Mr. Legge fell in love with her so ardently.

"As a hostess, Mrs. Legge had real genius. She sensed the type of hospitality and entertainment that would be particularly pleasing to her guests on each occasion. For a group of Harvester men from out in the field her dinners were simple and informal, calculated to put them at ease. Having spent years in Nebraska working in connection with the farm implement business, she could talk shop with them intelligently. She met them on their own ground. This delighted them. When she entertained the high officials of the company and their ladies, her dinners were appropriately formal. She was as much at home in this hostess rôle as in entertaining the salesmen and the collectors from the country.

"Many of the Legges' guests came unexpectedly. She never knew how many men her husband would bring home with him with only fifteen or twenty minutes' notice. Always she was prepared for these unexpected guests and received them with a sincere welcome. This involved good planning—and what a planner she was! Her reserve larder was stocked with delicious foods. She was never under the necessity of offering apologies. Her only anxiety was to make these casual guests feel how welcome they were. This was not a gesture; it was sincere.

"She kept her own social calendar clear so that she would be free to meet these irregular demands. Her husband's interests and comfort always came first on her schedule. For ten years, when we lived in Chicago not far from the Legge home, I watched this drama of wifely devotion.

"At first their house was furnished with massive pieces. She knew how unsuitable they were but offered only one word of comment—'Wait.' This remark was accompanied by a sly wink. Very gradually they were supplanted by pieces selected with excellent taste. Her husband came to be very proud of her knowledge of fine things. Once she laughingly confessed:

" 'When we were married Alex laid down the law: No oriental rugs; no evening dresses; no diamonds; no society stuff; no gimcrack furniture or furnishings.'

"She accepted this edict without protest and played the game as he dealt the cards. Then his own attitude changed. In Russia, he bought her some fine furs and would have given her diamonds, but she did not care for jewels. He would give her money on anniversaries with the hint that she might wish to spend it for something nice for the house. He went into homes that were beautifully furnished and decorated and came home with the feeling that his house was capable of improvement in certain particulars.

"I never knew a more generous person than Katherine Legge. But with every gift she gave more of herself than she did of money."

Mrs. Legge was of immeasurable service to Alex in his

European contacts, particularly with people of great importance who were highly sophisticated. He relied comfortably upon her social tact and her ability to meet situations with which he was unfamiliar.

It is certain that he was much more comfortable on many formal occasions because she was with him. He knew that she would learn in advance the social requirements of each situation and be prepared to help him meet it. He didn't surrender his individuality—that he could never do—but he had reached a sufficient appreciation of her tact and judgment to turn over to her the task of piloting him through situations beset with rocks and shoals of social formalism which could not be ignored.

Then, too, he counted upon her for help not purely social; he discussed with her the great problems with which he was dealing and attached much importance to her judgment and intuitions respecting them. She had an almost uncanny insight into human character. When she told him that she felt a certain man was not entirely to be trusted, he was inclined to "stop, look, and listen."

The men of Harvester's overseas staff were very practical "foreign trade diplomats" and they knew something of the extent to which their chief relied upon his wife's judgment, intuitions and hunches in meeting his problems both for the Harvester Company and for his Government.

Like Mr. Legge, she knew the Harvester organization, from office boys and young girls up to the top men. And she was interested in the youngsters, personally and collectively, and loved to talk about them and plan what might be done for them.

She had been a farm girl, country schoolteacher,

office worker, lawyer and business woman. To a great extent her experience paralleled that of her husband. They spoke the same language and were fundamentally democrats in the social meaning of the term. Her sympathies, like his, went out to farm people, village folk and those workers in industry whose interests were directly connected with farming. Thus the partnership between Alex Legge and his clever wife was an ideal one; they had majored in much the same subjects in the school of experience.

In a recent conversation, the late Cyrus H. McCormick remarked to the writer:

"My mother admired Katherine Legge immensely and I know the extent to which that feeling was reciprocated. Again, my first wife loved this remarkable woman devotedly. They both recognized that she was the supreme influence in Mr. Legge's life in his mature years. She was not only one of the most lovable of women but had a mentality that was a constant amazement to all of us who knew her.

"In view of the fact that her contacts with formal society had been limited before her marriage to Alex, many of her acquaintances were unable to account for her infallible social discrimination. The answer seems to me to be that it was a natural gift that came instantly into flower when it was needed. Her mind was highly acquisitive along social as well as business and intellectual lines. She did not need to observe a social practice more than once to grasp it and the reason for its observance.

"So it was with what she gleaned in conversation with her intimate women friends who were socially experienced. In a word, Mrs. Legge was not only naturally refined, but had a mind of peculiar penetration and vigor. I am happy to feel that my first wife was able to be of great help to Mrs. Legge. Their friendship was singularly close and intimate.

"We speak of Alex Legge as a 'self-made' man. Mrs. Legge was a 'self-made' woman. She went ahead on her own power. Her influence in the Harvester organization was very great. The Harvester men who were entertained in the Legge home took her to their hearts. Her devotion to her husband was reason enough for this. Their loyalty to him was unqualified and intense. When they became satisfied by personal observation that she was completely dedicated to advancing his interests, with no individual social ambition of her own to gratify, they accepted her as their ally.

"This feeling was intensified by the recognition that she had a mind that made her his natural mate. Then when they saw that her practical knowledge of business and of the farm implement industry was such that she could instantly grasp any point made by the ablest man in the service and react with observations of great shrewdness, they simply made her a member of their own lodge. This was a peculiar position for a woman to occupy. I do not think he ever deliberately went against her judgment and intuitions in any important business decision and she knew what he was doing all the time."

Learning His Way in the Foreign Field,
1908–1916

MR. CHARLES H. HANEY, now retired and living in Glendale, California, was for many years in charge of Harvester sales abroad.

"It was in 1902," says Mr. Haney, "when I was with the Deering Company and he with the McCormick Company, that I first met Mr. Legge—and that was in connection with the consolidation.

"His first trip to Europe was made with me in 1908. He felt quite superior because he was not seasick during the crossing. But when we arrived in London where we were to attend a banquet that evening, he became violently seasick. This was the first time he ever wore a silk hat. We all declared that the silk hat was just too much for him!

"We made an extended trip through Europe at that time—to Paris, Belgium, Germany, Sweden and Siberia —visiting the foreign branch offices. In Siberia we spent at least nineteen days on the train out of the thirty days we were there. Mr. Legge set a swift pace. For example, we arrived in Omsk, Siberia, about 3:00 a.m., snatched a few hours' sleep, went to the company offices where we spent the rest of the day and the next night, and then caught a 2:00 a.m. train out.

"But Mr. Legge was a tireless worker. He never spared himself—or others, for that matter. He had a marvelous memory for persons as well as things, knew an amazing number of people, what they did and their personal characteristics and circumstances.

"Then, too, he had a special faculty for picking men and fitting them to jobs. He seemed to know almost everyone in the organization and what each man could do best. These contacts were democratic to the last degree. He never gave the impression that he considered himself higher than anyone else. Even when he was president of the company, he worked out in the field in overalls whenever he got the chance. On one occasion up in Winnipeg, he was driving a bolt downward when it was met by another driven upward. At the meeting of the bolts the sparks and the language flew. The mechanic under the machine gave Alex Legge the grandest 'cussing' he had ever received since he had achieved high official position. But this did not injure the man's standing with the head of the company. On the contrary, it helped him. They became fast friends and Mr. Legge never failed to introduce this mechanic with a laughing reference to this incident."

"I have never met a man," related Henry Cowan, for many years stationed at Paris, representing Harvester's interests, "whom I considered a greater leader of men than Alex Legge; and it fell to my lot to meet some high generals over there. No man came over from the Harvester Company who was better loved than he. His wit was often sharp, but it left no wounds. Every man in the organization who came in contact with him was for him, heart and soul.

"Diplomacy is a great factor in human relations of every sort abroad. Let no one persuade you that Alex Legge was not a good diplomat on European soil. His American abruptness was not by any means bad diplomacy for he always brought it into play at just the right moment. Sitting in with a group of French politicians he could be just as diplomatic as they. Let someone crack a good joke and he would cap it with one as good or better. And he was an adept at listening to others, but he knew the moment to seize the situation.

"In Paris Mr. Legge told me this story about Lord Cecil who was conversing with a number of important Frenchmen. One of his own party asked him, 'Do you understand what they are saying?' Lord Cecil replied, 'Yes, what they are saying and what they are thinking.' Mr. Legge enjoyed this incident. It was, I think, descriptive of his own perceptions on many occasions.

"His dealings with branch managers who were years older than he called for business diplomacy of the highest order. This situation was sensitive. These men knew Europe and he did not. Many of them spoke several languages and enjoyed high social connections. They were very important in the Harvester service. He was not always satisfied with the way they were handling the business and he had ideas of his own to offer. The delicate task of putting these plans across to them was done by indirection—mainly by asking questions. What did they think of doing this or that, or making certain changes to improve conditions which they mentioned as being unsatisfactory? Only occasionally would he give a positive order. One of these was:

" 'Tell the men when they come back to America that they must not publicly discuss the things that are going on over here. Keep to the Harvester business; leave European political and public affairs out of it.'

"Illustrating his remarkable memory: He rarely carried any statistics on paper about with him but he could talk figures, costs, prices, turn-over and volume as readily as if he were reading them.

"He didn't overlook anyone in the service, from the least to the greatest. One day he asked how a certain man was getting along. He was told that the man seemed to be falling down on the job.

" 'How long has he been with the company?' asked Mr. Legge. The reply was, 'In France only a few years, but with the company about twenty years.'

"Mr. Legge grinned as he said, 'Seems to me it took you a long time to find out he was no good.'

"On another occasion he asked me: 'Henry, how is that young man you brought over from America progressing?'

"I answered, 'All right. There's only one thing wrong with him—he is too young.'

" 'Oh, hell!' laughed Mr. Legge. 'He'll soon grow out of *that*.'

"He introduced me to Mr. Hoover. They had a luncheon appointment with an important French official and Mr. Hoover did not show up. Mr. Legge later remarked to the future President of the United States: 'Herbert, why didn't you come to luncheon with that French official? I know! You get up in your room with a lot of damned statistics and forget that the world is turning around.'

"Mr. Legge had nicknames for all of us. He used to

call Mr. Haney 'the Bishop'; my predecessor, Mr. LaPorte, he named 'the Swiss Admiral.' He was full of odd whimsical quirks. For example:

"We were preparing a big implement show in Paris. Looking at the various machines in one exhibit, he saw a plow with a man-harness attached. 'Henry,' gleefully exclaimed Mr. Legge. 'Buy that plow for me, charge it to my personal account and send it over to me in America. I want to take it out to my Hinsdale farm so that the men who visit me there can see it. You know I put them all at work but most of them want to pull away from the job. This is just the thing for them!'

"I never knew a man who could stand as much punishment as Alex Legge. He rode in an open motor car in the coldest weather when any ordinary man could not have stood it. His resistance to cold and hardship was amazing. He was often called the 'Man of Iron.' He certainly deserved the title so far as his physical resistance was concerned. He enjoyed joking the men in the Paris office about not being able to lose sleep without showing it the next day. I recall that he told P. S. Botter, an Englishman who has been associated with the Harvester Company all his life, 'You and Cowan must be staying up late. You look sleepy and not able to work.' He could work all night and then keep right on going!"

Every man who was brought in from the country to the Chicago office exerted a peculiar pull upon the interest and sympathy of Alex Legge. He knew from experience how strange and confusing their new surroundings must seem to them. His desire to make these recruits from the territory feel comfortable and at home in the general offices was constantly in his thought. Of scores of incidents related by grateful recipients of this fatherly

THE AMERICAN "LEGGETT'S DEN" NEAR ROGERS, NEBRASKA

care, perhaps the experience of George Koenig will best serve to illustrate this unfailing sense of responsibility:

"Of course I was pleased to be promoted to the position of assistant to the foreign sales manager, Mr. Haney, whom I eventually succeeded. At first I felt like the proverbial cat in a strange garret. Out in the West we did things in our own way which was very different from the procedure in the Chicago office. I had been at headquarters for perhaps a month when I was summoned to Mr. Legge's room. I thought I was in for a calling-down.

"But the big boss greeted me genially and asked me if I had found an agreeable location. I explained that I was living at a small hotel for the reason that the man I was succeeding lived there and I wished to get all the pointers possible from him regarding my new job. Mr. Legge made no response and I was still wondering what was in the back of his mind when he remarked:

"'George, you'll have to get used to spending more money in Chicago than you've been spending down in the Southwest, and you may as well make up your mind to do it cheerfully. When I first came to Chicago I was in the same boat that you are in now. I was alone a whole lot and loved to read, but hated to spend money for books. So I haunted the second-hand book stores. There was a certain book I wanted, the regular price of which was a dollar. I found a copy of it in a second-hand place at fifty cents. I felt real thrifty when I took the book and the half dollar in change that the clerk gave me and went on to luncheon. The cashier at the restaurant returned the half dollar to me with the remark that it was counterfeit. I might just as well have paid the dollar for the book at a first-class bookstore at the start.'

"Now that wasn't much of a yarn in itself, but it

accomplished its purpose of putting me at my ease. Then he told me that I was to feel free to come to his office and talk with him about anything that was on my mind relating to the business or to my personal situation. And he added: 'If I can help you, I will.' That was Alex Legge. That was his attitude toward all the men, particularly those from the country and unfamiliar with the methods of headquarters. Is it any wonder that we all loved the ground he walked on?

"Mr. Legge never made me mad but once. I had worked for the McCormick Company many years before the Harvester Company was formed and knew that the first commandment in the decalogue of the organization was that all business must be open and aboveboard. This had been thoroughly instilled into us. While Mr. Legge was on the War Industries Board all purchases by any of the foreign governments required his approval. All purchases by any foreign government of Harvester products were turned over to men having no connection with our company. Mr. Legge would not even discuss such business.

"After the close of the War, the French government entered the market for a very large purchase of products in our line for use in rehabilitation. All of our competitors were after this big order. I succeeded in getting the greater part of this business and felt that, in doing so, I had achieved a master stroke for the company.

"Not long after I returned to Chicago, Mr. Legge unexpectedly made a flying trip from Washington to the Harvester headquarters. He entered my office, closed the door, and turned his boring eyes upon me. His excitement was evident. He shot one question at me and it was this: 'George, is that business from the French straight and clean?'

"I was mad all the way through and didn't hesitate to tell him so. Finally he checked my outburst, grinned and remarked, 'Oh, forget it! That was a big block of business —more than I thought you would be able to get. I was sure it was straight, but I just wanted you to tell me so.'

"When Mr. Legge was abroad, he worked the boys pretty hard. He himself worked from early in the morning until late at night. As he didn't sleep well, he tried to keep us all up with him. When he got ready to leave London at the close of one of those strenuous sessions, the boys said, 'Well, Mr. Legge, we have enjoyed your visit immensely; but for God's sake, don't miss the boat!'

"When Mr. Legge would leave one of the branch offices, he would have everything in good shape; but on the boat he had afterthoughts and when he got to a certain point on the ocean, he always thought of something he might possibly have forgotten, and we were sure to get a message. Once, when he was leaving Paris, the boys said: 'Well, Mr. Legge, we suppose we'll hear from you when you get to your pet meridian.'

"We did! And the boys sent him a message saying that they had assumed he would cable, but the matter had already been attended to."

Mr. Legge's vision of the foreign field was so comprehensive as to astonish the Harvester men who had spent years in its development. Wherever he went—and he traveled widely throughout the Old World—he made contacts with leading financiers, bankers, government financial men and economists, and officials of the departments of agriculture of the various countries. Always he was searching for those regions that offered the greatest opportunity for new development, expansion and improvement.

This quest for new worlds to conquer yielded him a rich harvest of excitement and pleasure. He felt the thrill of expanding his mental horizon to limits of which he had not dreamed as a Wyoming cowboy or a collector of farm machinery accounts in Nebraska. His acquisitive mind responded eagerly to the challenge of countries and regions offering opportunities for agricultural advancement by the aid of modern agricultural implements. His keen eyes scanned a world in which absurdly ancient methods of agriculture still prevailed, where harvests could be multiplied many fold by the general use of the tillage and harvest tools made in the plants that he controlled.

No one, however, who knew Alex Legge's mind and heart will challenge the statement that his thought was not alone of the number of machines to be sold in these undeveloped regions. His big thrill was in the thought of what supplanting obsolete agricultural methods and tools would mean to the common people in multiplied harvests and food supplies, in liberation from conditions of slavery. Like Abraham Lincoln's, his thought was for the "common people"; white, black, brown or yellow, they were human beings and workers. It was great to be in a business that could not fail to improve human living conditions as a natural result of its extension. The thought of this collateral or incidental benefaction was always in the back of his mind.

He rarely talked about it and then only casually to one or two intimates. It was, however, his religion—something not to be discussed but to be lived.

The sharp contrasts which he found in Old World agricultural methods and conditions vividly dramatized this viewpoint for him and made his personal contacts with agriculture in foreign countries interesting and exciting.

His fundamental democracy and his shrewd and comprehensive grasp of economic principles compelled him to a broader appreciation of the relation between the abundance of food supplies from "the good earth" and the welfare of all the people in any country. The people of the soil—they were his people, anywhere and everywhere, the world over! He looked upon every farm machine placed on the soil of a backward country as a missionary of a new abundance of food and clothing, a liberator from the chains of agricultural serfdom.

Probably his patience in listening to arguments which seemed fatuous and "talky" was prompted by a desire not to chill free expression. He had no use for "yes men" in any rank in the organization. Sometimes this consideration presented difficulties and called into play his peculiar kind of diplomacy. An example in point is given by his nephew, Roy Legge, head of the motor truck branch of the International Harvester Company in San Francisco.

"When I was only a young lad and living with Uncle Alex in his Chicago home," relates this nephew, "he was kind enough to ask me to go along with him and a party of men from the works to witness a rather important field demonstration of new and improved models of Harvester machines. Of course I was flattered, but I kept my ears open and my lips closed. The men talked much on the way out to the testing grounds, particularly two of them who seemed eager to air their technical theories in the presence of the big boss.

"I had a feeling that Uncle Alex didn't enjoy what the two leaders of the conversation were saying and that something was going to happen shortly. It did! In a very casual way, as if simply changing the subject, he laughingly remarked: 'The other day I ran across a rhyme that struck me as being rather good. It runs this way:

> "'A wise old owl sat on an oak.
> The more he saw the less he spoke;
> The less he spoke the more he heard.
> Why aren't you like that wise old bird?'

"One of the two men who had overtalked exclaimed, 'Great!'—but both dropped into silence. However, Uncle Alex occasionally drew them into the general conversation that followed. They gave no indication that they felt hurt by the rhyme he had repeated. But the point of it certainly got across to them!"

In defining the relationships of big business, formal contracts are as basic as legal statutes. The larger the business organization, the greater the extent to which this formalism prevails. While Alex Legge generally respected this practice of having contracts drawn in strict legal terminology, he was entirely capable of brushing aside this traditional practice when circumstances seemed to require it.

In a casual meeting with W. B. Freeman, head of the Pacific Implement Company, they arrived at the conclusion that a certain business relationship between their companies would be of mutual advantage. Mr. Legge was sure that this would be the case. He did not wish to "scare the hen off the nest" by calling in a lawyer. Therefore he scribbled their agreement upon a scrap of paper which happened to be at hand at the moment. It was the most informal of documents but it expressed their mutual understanding as clearly as if it had been couched in the most formal and elaborate legal phraseology.

For five or six years this simple document governed the relations of the two contracting companies. The business which it covered amounted to many thousands of dollars. But repeatedly this scribbled agreement was a stumbling block to a succession of auditors who viewed it as a mere memorandum for a contract. The answer to each surprised auditor was:

"That's the contract. It's in Alex Legge's own hand—and it stands. Mr. Freeman has never challenged it. It holds just as firmly as if it were four pages long and had been drawn up by skilled lawyers."

Perhaps a more discriminating summary of Alex Legge's great qualities of heart and mind has never been made than that of the late Cyrus H. McCormick in an unforgettable conversation with the writer:

"Mr. Legge's sense of justice," remarked Mr. McCormick, "was to me his most conspicuous quality. Always his first concern was to see that every man with whom he had relations, in the Harvester organization and outside of it, received full justice at his hands. His honesty was forthright and blunt, never side-stepping anything. His directness was unswerving and he went straight to the heart of every question. Often I have heard his associates remark, 'He always hits the bull's eye, whether we want to agree with what he says or not.' His judgment and bluntness made an individual of him—took him out of any class or group.

"His way of judging men always interested me. He first considered them as to character, then as to ability. I observed this very carefully and with great admiration. Of course he took into consideration experience and judgment as well as character and native ability. My mother, Nettie Fowler McCormick, admired Mr. Legge tremendously. Repeatedly I have heard her remark, 'Whatever Mr. Legge says is law.' She felt that he could not make a serious mistake—a small one, yes, but not a fundamental and important one. Let me add that I never knew him to make a big mistake.

"He conquered everyone by the soundness of his judgment. His leadership was quickly recognized in any gathering of men, regardless of their importance in the industrial, financial or political world. This leadership was as natural to him as it was to Abraham Lincoln. He was strikingly like Lincoln in many respects, but at the moment I am thinking of his marvelous gift of common sense, his ability to push aside a confusion of unimportant details and go straight to the point of any problem. His abhorrence of ostentation and formalism was Lincolnesque to a marked degree. He loved simplicity and held to it under all circumstances.

"He was most like Lincoln, I think, in his great human sympathy for all mankind, regardless of social strata. Of course Mr. Legge had faults, being a very human man, but they were inconsequential. The greatness of his heart, of his character and of his ability instantly dismissed trivial faults from consideration. My feeling is that this country has not produced another man so like Abraham Lincoln in great qualities of heart and mind as Alexander Legge. They had, too, many of the same minor traits and little eccentricities.

"Mr. Legge was profoundly and eagerly interested in the welfare of all who worked for the company and he devised and established the most important features of the company's welfare work for its employees."

Alex Legge was full of odd whimsies. The passing of the horse-and-buggy days brought out his sympathy for those who must suffer from the mechanical advancement in private transportation. This leader in the mechanization of agriculture could not resist the appeal of the automobile. It pained him, however, to see carriage manufacturers crowded into the ditch of disaster by these horseless vehicles. He felt that he must have an automobile but determined to make a kindly gesture in the direction of the manufacturer who had made buggies and carriages for him.

He sent to the Staver factory an automobile engine with instructions to build a body to accommodate the mechanism. This was done and the result somewhat resembled a mogul freight locomotive. It commanded both attention and right-of-way. He had given the work to the Staver company as an expression of good-will and to "help out" when orders for buggies were dropping to the vanishing point.

Although Scotch to the core, Alex Legge had small patience with the golf-players in the organization, or outside of it. His usual comment on golf-playing was: "If you want exercise, dig a post hole! That's useful."

He observed many new devices that offended his keen sense of thrift by reason of their astonishing popularity. Radios, for example, were being bought by the millions on credit by those who could not, in his opinion, afford them. In the slang of the day, these devices became his "pet peeve." He seldom missed an opportunity to express his hostile opinion of these instruments of entertainment and of those who bought them. His disapproval of them was as strong as Old Sandy's hostility to the cottage organ —"a kist o' whussles" which he declared should not enter his house. He refused to have a radio in his house although his wife confessed that she would enjoy one. An intimate friend says that he was on the point of presenting her with one just before her fatal illness. After her death, he would not have one in his house.

Alex Legge was never content in the metropolitan environment of Chicago after his marriage. A big city might be all right for a bachelor whose only recreation was incessant mental work; but it was no place in which to have a real home. He craved country life where he could have daily contact with the soil, get out of doors and dig and plant and work off steam, according to the habit of his earlier years.

Mr. Legge became increasingly restless and this feeling was aggravated by rides into the country with W. M. Gale, then secretary of the company and for many years one of his most intimate friends. Mr. Gale had a few acres of wooded land on the banks of the DuPage River near Wheaton. As early as 1912, Mr. Legge began to visit this sylvan spot with Mr. Gale and soon committed himself to finding a desirable place in the country.

This was the beginning of a long series of scouting expeditions. The Hinsdale section especially appealed to Mr. Legge because of its natural beauty and its easy accessibility to Chicago.

He entered on this quest with the intention of getting only a small place, perhaps five or six acres, an adequate site for a dignified and attractive country house and elbow room for exercise. In their adventurings they explored the property of the estate of the late Enos M. Barton. Its beautiful rolling landscape charmed Alex Legge. This was what he wanted! But he would be obliged to wait until this large estate was released for subdivision. This occurred in 1916, and he bought fifty-three acres.

The development of the Hinsdale estate began shortly after its purchase with the building of a large garage having commodious living quarters for the help on its second floor. A small cottage for the ultimate accommodation of the gardener was next constructed and was immediately occupied as a week-end retreat by Mr. and Mrs. Legge. They had great pleasure in planning and furnishing it so that it might serve as a place for entertaining their undiminished procession of guests, all eager to see the new estate.

As Mr. Legge insisted upon spending every available moment on the grounds, the little cottage was crowded to capacity every week-end. These pre-war days undoubtedly were the happiest in the married life of Alex and Katherine Legge. She was entirely equal to the problems of entertainment in a cottage of almost miniature dimensions. The dining table occupied almost the entire area of the dining room. Small benches, each accommodating two persons, served in place of chairs and required much less space. Not many meals were served in this little cottage for fewer than fourteen guests. The cooking was mainly done in the town house by the Japanese servant, and taken out in hampers to the little cottage.

The only criticism of their entertainment in the minds of their men guests related to the standing expectation that, without regard to their rank in the financial or political world, they would join their host in physical labor upon the grounds. He set them a stiff pace. Many of these guests left with lame backs, sore muscles, and a greater admiration for the physical powers of their host than for his ideas of recreation.

Eventually it developed that, to Mr. Legge, this was in the nature of an interesting character test of his guests and that when he found one who had the courage bluntly to decline to match physical endurance with this farm-raised giant, he commanded his host's respect.

America's entry into the World War, April 6, 1917, made the immediate organization of American industries into a vast war machine a paramount necessity. Alex Legge's summons to help in this huge task was as inevitable as its acceptance. The war ended his dream of a stately house that was to be to him and his wife a "real home." The plans for it were drawn and approved. During the war private building was banned as an unpatriotic diversion of materials and labor from war use; after the war, their costs were prohibitive, at least to a thrifty Scot. Therefore it was not built. About 1921, the Legges took a large house in Hinsdale village where they continued to entertain until 1924.

XI

War Industries Board,
1917–1918

H OW Alex Legge was called from comparative obscurity to the war-time service of his country in which he became a towering international figure is best told by Bernard M. Baruch who summoned him to his great task.

"When the Inter-Allied Purchasing Commission was established in August, 1917," relates Mr. Baruch, "I was at the head of the Raw Materials Division of the War Industries Board, and became one of the three members of that commission. The first step was to find an able and experienced industrialist to act as my right-hand man. Getting the right man was tremendously important. Hundreds of inquiries had been sent out to leaders in all lines of industry. With the late Leland Summers, I was going through a stack of cards compiled from the answers to our questionnaires. Suddenly he pointed to the name of Alex Legge on a dozen of the cards and exclaimed:

"'There's your man! He knows Europe, knows human nature, is a shrewd trader, as straight as a die and an unbeatable fighter. His is the best mind in the International

Harvester Company—but I don't think you can get him.'

"'Never heard of him!' I exclaimed.

"But I knew Summers too well not to play his hunch. His fund of information was so comprehensive that we called him 'the human Britannica.' At my request, Mr. Cyrus H. McCormick came on for a conference. He was momentarily aghast at the thought of losing Legge from the Harvester organization at so critical a time. But, being a sound patriot, he frankly admitted that I had spotted the best possible man for the place; that Legge had a positive genius for sound judgment; that he knew the whole foreign trade field almost as intimately as the domestic field; that he had unflinching courage, prodigious personal industry and endurance and a rare ability to inspire the confidence and loyalty of others. One interview with Alex Legge himself when he came on, and he was instantly drafted as my chief of staff. Later he became general manager of the Inter-Allied Purchasing Commission.

"In 1918, when I was appointed chairman of the War Industries Board, I drafted Alex Legge as vice chairman. Soon afterward I wrote him a letter delegating to him all the authority that President Wilson had conferred on me so that there would be no possibility of even a momentary interruption of the steady flow of war supplies to the fighting front and to the Allies. Positive authority to decide instantly was necessary on that job. President Wilson had given me complete authority so far as that task was concerned—all that he himself possessed—and this I passed on to Alex for use when required.

"To me, the man in the high post of authority is always the vital consideration. So I have consistently studied men as the main problem in every large undertaking.

In facing this task I realized that my quest was to be no hunt for laurel-crowned heads, for acclaimed kings of industry with years of great achievement behind them; that only the younger men in whom the red blood of courage and the urge of initiative were running strong could do this almost superhuman job. They must be fighters and diplomats, good salesmen as well as good executives. Lack of a national reputation was no handicap. On these lines Alex Legge was unhesitatingly selected."

The World War marked the most vital and dramatic period of Alex Legge's life. His personal development in it was amazing. He revealed his mental powers in a way to command the confidence and co-operation of the foremost statesmen, diplomats, economists, international financiers and industrialists of the world.

This he achieved without a change in the technique by which he had developed his leadership in the International Harvester Company. He remained the simple, picturesque, unpretentious Alex Legge in the War Industries Board and in the historic international councils at Paris that he had been on the prairies of Nebraska, the cattle range of Wyoming and in the early executive meetings of the McCormick Company.

Probably no other man of his day equipped with so limited an academic education ever exerted greater influence upon the financial and economic affairs of the world than this son of pioneer conditions in Wisconsin and Nebraska. What he did and how he did it is one of the most stirring epics of American individualism.

The public rather generally rated Baruch as "just a Wall Street speculator"—an odd choice, it was thought, for the master of the industries of America in the great war emergency. Why had not the President picked a trained industrialist who knew industry's problems and spoke its language? The fact is that Baruch had organized several large and successful industrial concerns and was an outstanding industrialist of the creative type. Realizing the futility of attempting to modify this common impression by explaining that it had been years since the fluctuations of the market had been his bread and butter dependence, he silently accepted the brand of "Wall Street speculator" and chose Alex Legge, thoroughbred industrialist, as an answer to this prevailing criticism.

What a marvelous team those two made! Baruch, polished, serene, sophisticated, smiling; Legge, awkward, brusque, aggressive, and rough as a shagbark hickory. There was, however, the same tough resilient fiber in both. For all his patience, smiles and poise, Baruch was as unyielding as Legge. Backing to the limit the forces fighting Germany was the supreme consideration. Everything else had to yield to it.

When Legge's appointment was announced a solicitous friend of Baruch's asked him, "Have you stopped to think that Legge will get away with this job—along with all of the credit for it?"

"Good!" answered Baruch. "I hope he does. I'll still have the credit of having picked him, and that will be enough for me."

"President Wilson," relates Baruch, "once remarked that two kinds of men came to Washington—the kind that swelled and the kind that grew. Alex Legge was the best representative of the second class. He grew and flowered and brought forth fruit that gave strength and confidence to all who worked with him."

A glance at the background of the War Industries Board is essential here. Before the powder magazine of

ALEX LEGGE AND HAROLD F. McCORMICK (RIGHT) WATCHING TEST OF AN EXPERIMENTAL MOTOR CULTIVATOR, 1919

Central Europe exploded, there existed a popular rather than a governmental organization known as the Industrial Preparedness Committee. Largely through its endeavors the Military Appropriations Act was passed in August, 1916, creating a Council of National Defense. Then followed an Advisory Commission of this Council, its members appointed by the President. The United States had not then severed relations with Germany, but plans were being worked out in Washington to prepare for the worst. Here entered Bernard Baruch. This Advisory Commission was the real agency in making ready for war. It created its War Industries Board July 8, 1917. With the Inter-Allied Purchasing Commission—a collateral arm for handling the problems of supplies to the Allies and neutrals—it held the high throne of authority and power.

In a letter to Baruch, the President defined the War Industries Board as "a civilian agency co-operating with the Army and Navy for the control and direction of Industry to war needs and purposes." Complete co-operation was imperative—voluntary if possible, involuntary if necessary.

The definite dimensions of the job which Alex Legge undertook under Baruch are described by Grosvenor B. Clarkson in his "Industrial America in the World War," published by Houghton Mifflin Company in 1923:

1. To allocate commodities of which there is or is likely to be a deficit; to encourage their increased production and effect their orderly flow "into channels most conducive to the purposes of war" which necessitates "priority" and price-fixing determinations.
2. To analyze, bring together, measure, alter and restrain the demands of the Government, of the Allies, and of the public.
3. To ascertain to what extent and in what manner the supplies could meet the requirements; and to take the action thereby indicated.

A staggering task—but it was not in Mr. Baruch, Alex Legge or their associates to admit that anything that had to be done could not be accomplished. The members of the Board were:

Bernard M. Baruch, Chairman
Alexander Legge, Vice Chairman
Rear Admiral F. F. Fletcher, Navy
Brigadier General Hugh S. Johnson, Army
    (Succeeded September, 1918, by Major General George
    W. Goethals)
Robert S. Brookings, Chairman Price-Fixing Committee
Hugh Frayne, Labor
Edwin B. Parker, Priorities Commissioner
George N. Peek, Commissioner of Finished Products
J. Leonard Replogle, Steel Administrator
L. L. Summers, Technical Adviser
Albert C. Ritchie, General Counsel
Howard P. Ingels, Secretary
Herbert Bayard Swope, Associate Member
Clarence Dillon, Harrison Williams, and Harold T. Clark,
    Assistants to the Chairman.

Mr. Legge, according to Clarkson, had the Requirements Division, the Clearance Office, the Allied Purchasing Commission, certain raw materials sections, a number of other sections and the special advisory committee on plants and munitions—all these in addition to his work as vice chairman of the Board, second in command to Mr. Baruch. The main groups appearing before the Board were:

The Supply Departments of Army and Navy, each having a
    representative
The General Staff of Army and Navy
The Emergency Fleet Corporation (Shipping Board)
The Allied Purchasing Commission
The Red Cross
The Railroad Administration
The Food Administration
The Marine Corps
All the Industries of America

Before we entered the World War American industrialists had been prosecuted and punished, under the Sher-
man Anti-Trust Act, for getting together on anything
affecting prices. Suddenly they were ordered to organize
into groups, like companies and regiments, so that they
could respond to war demands with unity and military
precision.

Up to the hour when President Wilson realized that
our entry into the World War was inevitable, the industrialists of this country had rejoiced in their rugged independence. They had always stood squarely on their own
feet and fought their own battles. That was the American
thing to do, as they understood it. They were not senti-
mentalists; they talked little about "ideals" or "patriotism." To them business was a very practical matter of
profit-getting and profit-keeping—and a World War
looked to them a rich harvest ready for the cutting!

Their forebears, who had conquered the wilderness
and made America the greatest industrial nation on earth,
had fought it out on these individualistic lines, and they
had themselves lived by the same rugged code. This was
the "American tradition," and they were proud of it.

They would have resented any implication that they
were not patriotic. They felt a vast and glowing satisfaction in the greatness of their country, in its enormous resources, its beneficent institutions, and the spirit of its
people. They endowed colleges and hospitals, and became generous founders of worthy institutions. Who could
challenge their patriotism?

But they held stoutly to the doctrine of unrestricted
self-determination. No man or group of men in Washington or elsewhere could tell them "where to get on or
where to get off," or interfere with their free management
of their enterprises "without due process of law!" That

was undeniably the attitude and temper of the industrialists of this country as a whole.

Naturally, it was difficult for them instantly to adjust themselves to an abrupt reversal of their relationships with each other and with their government.

A more difficult task than that of changing this viewpoint to one of accepting orders from Washington as to what they must or must not do could not be suggested. Their imagination was not equal to its comprehension or acceptance. The idea was un-American and revolutionary!

The first task which confronted Baruch and Legge was to inventory the material and human resources of industrial America. "Never before," says Clarkson, "was there such a focusing of knowledge of the vast fields of American industry, commerce and transportation. Never was there such an approach to omniscience in the business affairs of a continent."

The sessions of the War Industries Board have been likened to New England town meetings. For intimacy, yes; but for intensity the most acrimonious town meeting ever held in New England was a pious love-feast compared with sessions in which automobile manufacturers, for example, contended for enough iron, steel and men to keep their industry alive.

Proceedings were almost scandalously informal; everyone who appeared was free to speak his mind without restraint; but he had to take, in the same spirit, what Baruch and Legge gave. This freedom of expression relieved the pressure and carried the conviction that these two men at the head of the table, like their colleagues, would be fair, reasonable and absolutely patriotic.

In the early days of the War Industries Board there were many problems of overlapping functions. For example, there were two materials—cordage and jute—in which the Food Administration was as much interested as the War Industries Board. Baruch and Legge went together to see Food Administrator Hoover. Legge did most of the talking. The situation was complicated. Hoover was being pressed on every side. After listening for some time Hoover said, "Take the damn things and we will set up liaison officers with you!" As Legge and Baruch were moving out of the door, Legge chuckled and said, "That's the way to fix it, Boss. He got rid of a tough one—but there aren't as many quills on that porcupine as he thinks!"

The march of events in Alex Legge's war service is best seen through the eyes of his colleagues who were most intimately associated with him in this vital and stirring period. Their recollections constitute a vivid panoramic picture of this unique man in action under the most trying responsibilities that could be imagined. They were in a position daily to witness and measure his startling penetration of mind, his prodigious industry, his unwavering courage, his fine human sympathy, his unsparing devotion to his country, his acute sense of fairness and his ability to lead men—which is the ultimate in diplomacy.

In the earlier sessions of the War Industries Board, General Hugh S. Johnson represented the War Department, reporting to General Goethals. He seldom if ever missed a session. Recently, talking of Alex Legge, he said:

"Despite the fact that his formal education was very meager, he had as complete a knowledge of world economics as any man who helped to solve the big problems that came with the World War. I speak carefully when I say that he was one of the greatest practical economists this country has ever produced.

"Perhaps his most Lincolnesque characteristic was his ability instantly to illuminate any situation with a story that fitted the circumstances perfectly.

"At a certain meeting, after the War was over, it was proposed to form a War Industries Board Association. Alex asked the privilege of telling a story about a man who was dynamiting fish in one of the streams out in his own country. The man was followed, he said, by a small boy who had at his heels a little dog. The man threw a stick of dynamite and the dog, being a retriever, instantly went after it. Of course the dog was blown to pieces. With tears streaming down his face, the boy went about gathering up the fragments—a leg here and a bone there— and placed them in a pile. He stared at the remains of his pet for some time, and then solemnly remarked to the man: 'Well, as a dog, I guess he ain't much good anymore.' As Alex told that yarn, I could almost see Abraham Lincoln in his place.

"Regardless of how many men were on the War Industries Board and its subsidiaries, make no mistake as to the fact that the power rested in eight men—Admiral Fletcher, Robert Brookings, Hugh Frayne, Edwin Parker, George Peek, J. Leonard Replogle, L. L. Summers and myself— with Baruch and Alex Legge at their head, and that these men controlled the industries of the United States as they have never before or since been controlled. I have good reason for saying that President Wilson depended more on these men for carrying the war to a successful conclusion than upon any other group or body.

"There had been a lot of talk about the fierce scuffles that took place in the sessions of the War Industries Board and Baruch decided that it would be a good thing to stage a harmony demonstration to offset this impression. So, one day, the heads of all the emergency units were invited to attend.

"I represented the War Department and we wanted an increased supply of shells. The need was desperate. Alex had one besetting complex: that of taking care of the little fellow. He was besieged by an army of owners of relatively small machine shops begging for a chance to make shells. There were great numbers of these fellows and they worked upon Legge's sympathies until they finally convinced him that a practical plan for their participation could be devised.

"Of course I said that the scheme was crazy and Baruch backed me with the statement that it was the duty of the War Industries Board to see that the War Department got what it wanted and when it wanted it, regardless of any other consideration. Alex exploded at this. He certainly did burn me up! The harmony demonstration ended in one of the hottest brawls we ever had.

"One of the most amusing scenes I ever witnessed was the reception of the Italian delegation which was headed by Count V. Macchi di Cellere, followed by every person connected with the embassy—all in full dress uniform and wearing a dazzling array of medals and ribbons. For a moment I wondered how Alex would greet this very formal procession. But he was not at a loss for an instant. With a genial smile, he exclaimed, 'Welcome, sunny Italy!' He could not have given a more winning or fortunate greeting if he had made a formal and studied speech.

"It happened that the Italians wanted a big shipment of wheat which Alex was obliged to deny them. But this refusal made no difference in the attitude of the ambassador. After the 'sunny Italy' incident, the ambassador would take anything from Alex— even his remark after the famous Italian retreat of Caporetto: 'Say, Excellency, when are you fellows going to stop running and go to fighting?'

"I have seen Alex, when considering a very difficult problem, sit for a long time with his chin in his hand, his eyes looking dreamy. Suddenly he would exclaim, 'Here's my conclusion!' It might sound wild at the moment but time would prove that he was right.

"In a fight of any sort he was one of the toughest, and had a tongue like a mule-skinner's lash when he felt he had need to use it. Probably some people think that my language is rough; I'm just an amateur compared with Alex Legge when he let loose, but his sympathies were with all toilers, especially with tillers of the soil. This was his strongest complex—which is proved by the fact that he gave about a million dollars of his fortune, after providing generously for the surviving members of his family, to the Farm Foundation for the continued and systematic study of farm problems. He was a farmer and the friend of all farmers to the end of his days."

Because Howard P. Ingels was Secretary of the War Industries Board from its inception and therefore obliged to attend its every session, his knowledge of Alex Legge's activities in that body was peculiarly intimate and comprehensive. They were first associated in the work of the old Munitions Board.

"He was always for direct action without pussy-footing or evasion," says Mr. Ingels. "All personalities looked alike to him. He treated every problem with only one idea in mind: how to get supplies and equipment across to our soldiers and our Allies with the utmost promptness.

"I recall one meeting of the Board given over to searching and heated discussions as to whether certain of our

Allies were diverting their steel to domestic manufacture for non-war purposes, at the same time taking all the steel from us they could get for the manufacture of munitions, ships and other war equipment. Some of the Board members present evidently were inclined to feel that we must not press the Allies too hard on problems of this kind. Finally Alex arose at the head of the table and demanded:

" 'For God's sake, when are you fellows going to get some backbone and quit allowing these so-called Allies of ours to put this sort of thing over on us?'

"Instantly Alex demonstrated his leadership. All those who were eager to get things done naturally gravitated to him, knowing they could get quick action from him. His brutally frank manner won everybody to him. It was the best possible kind of diplomacy, for it inspired complete confidence.

"It is wellnigh impossible to convey a picture of what those sessions of the War Industries Board were like. They had no antecedent in history so far as I know. Their decisions were important to the whole world beyond the possibility of exaggeration—yet the only record was the very brief, skeleton-like notes which I made as secretary.

"Many an industry was represented in our sessions by groups of the ablest corporation lawyers in the country. Mr. Legge would listen patiently to their arguments with half-closed eyes. Suddenly he would interrupt and remark, 'As I understand it, this is what you are driving at.' Then he would state with graphic clearness the position of each group and give his opinion of the attitude of the War Industries Board. In this way he saved hours of time. He made his kindly spirit and his great reasonableness felt by all.

"Of course it was a matter of continually saying 'No' to

someone, and that negative usually implied the sacrifice of personal or corporation profits. But his negatives were invariably delivered in a manner to carry conviction as to their reasonableness in relation to War conditions and necessities. His denials, however, were made in a manner that left no doubt as to their finality. He didn't temporize, string any problem along or hold out false hopes. His decisions were as immediate and conclusive as the raps of an auctioneer's hammer.

"It was a time when men's nerves were on edge. Upon his decisions hung opportunities for huge profits. For example, there were many instances where the re-allocation of raw materials was necessary. At the outset certain raw materials had been allocated to private industries. Later developments compelled the recall of portions of these allotments. This involved the sacrifice of profits. Mr. Legge played this difficult rôle of 'Indian giver' with consummate tact. When he finished the explanation of the war circumstances which made this course necessary, the result was understanding and conviction in the minds of those industrialists to whom he delivered these almost crushing disappointments. His ability to inspire patriotic co-operation and disarm criticism was one of his greatest gifts.

"Alex Legge had a peculiar type of self-confidence. It was unconscious and without egotism. He simply thought straight to the heart of any problem and expressed his conclusions without hesitation, fear or favor. Thus, even his great courage was virtually unconscious. Recognition of the facts of any problem and the common sense deductions from them, crystallized into a practical course of action, did not, I think, call upon him for any conscious exercise of courage. His sense of modesty was very rare in a man of abilities so great as his."

When asked to recommend the right man to serve as commissioner of Finished Products on the Board, Legge unhesitatingly named George N. Peek.

"A picture of the War Industries Board in action ought to be preserved," declares Mr. Peek, "for it was a unique body and the most powerful and important civil group involved in the support of the World War. Its operations were led by two of the most remarkable men brought to the front by the great war crises.

"One conspicuous factor of Alex Legge's equipment for his great responsibilities on the War Industries Board was his intimate and comprehensive knowledge of conditions in all the different countries involved. This had been gained by years of first-hand observation and experience. He had been over the ground until he was as familiar with it as with his own Nebraska country. It is my conviction that in this feature of equipment for his job, he was unapproached by any of his colleagues.

"The Board transacted a tremendous volume of business. It had two regular meetings a week at eleven in the morning. If any member was absent when the meeting opened, he simply missed what had been done before his entry, because nothing was repeated. Each submitted in advance a memorandum of the subjects he wished to offer for discussion. These suggestions constituted the definite order of business. After it had been disposed of, Chairman Baruch went around the table and asked each member present if there were any other problems he would like to have threshed out in open discussion. Always there were plenty of them—and hot ones, too!

"I do not recall a single instance where a subject was thrown into this open forum without immediately bringing forward, without hesitation or fumbling, sound, definite and illuminating responses. And these problems were generally tough nuts to crack. The mental readiness of the members of the Board to meet these complex and often highly technical problems always impressed me as being extraordinary. We were dealing with the great World War and the decisions of the Board involved tremendous consequences. Getting the right viewpoint on each of these problems was, of course, the important thing and in this particular Baruch and Legge demonstrated their leadership in an amazing degree.

"Both Baruch and Alex Legge played the same system when any complaint involving the conduct or attitude of any member was brought forward. The invariable answer of either would be, 'Before you start, I am going to call in the man you are complaining about.' And this would be done. The result was that the chairman and the vice chairman of the Board had the implicit confidence of every member. And don't imagine for a moment that there were not plenty of complaints!

"I think the secret of how the Board accomplished its results so expeditiously was that both Baruch and Legge delegated their whole authority to each individual member, so far as that individual's particular responsibility was concerned.

"Mr. Legge had direct charge of all raw materials excepting steel. I was commissioner of Finished Products. We used to scrap about what were raw materials and what were finished products—often a complex and important problem. For example, when it became necessary for us to discuss wool, I insisted that it was a raw material and belonged to Alex Legge. He replied, 'No; the sheep is the raw material; its wool is your responsibility. Cattle belong in the raw material class and the hides and leather are finished products—and you get them!'

"This sort of thing was going on constantly. Everybody on the Board was supposed to be an authority in his own particular bailiwick of responsibility and there was a general understanding that he would defend his ideas to the last ditch. Responsibility always carried with it authority in the Board's system of operation.

"Baruch's and Legge's unfailing sense of humor repeatedly saved the day when there was a clash between them. For example, on one occasion, Alex showed an embarrassing degree of feeling on a certain point in contention. Finally Baruch exclaimed, 'In taking your position, Alex, you entirely lose sight of my nationality.'

"Instantly Legge answered: 'I don't forget your nationality for a moment. But you forget that my people came from Scotland, the only country on the globe in which your people can't make a living!'

"The tension was at once relieved by the laugh that followed.

"Alex could not tolerate delays that seemed to him unnecessary. A suspicion that red tape was holding up important war business infuriated him. Occasionally he resorted to extreme measures in breaking up a traffic jam of this sort. We had contracts with the imperial Russian government, then one of the Allies, involving the use of certain plants for the manufacture of munitions. When the Czar's government collapsed, these contracts had to be terminated and settled and perhaps new ones provided to make the facilities of the plants still available to us and to the Allies. This matter was handled by the State Department, and, eventually, by the Treasury Department. There it stuck and the Board could get no action from the assistant secretary of the Treasury who had it in charge.

"Finally, Legge's patience gave out, and he wrote to

that official to this effect: 'Permit me to suggest, my dear Mr. Secretary, that better men than you or I have faced the firing line for less serious offences than you are committing by delaying the clearing up of these plants.'

"Quite promptly he received in reply a pointed rebuke. Alex laughed when he showed me this letter and remarked: 'He certainly gave me hell—but I got those contracts cleared up!'

"Alex and I were agreed that it was impossible to do satisfactory business with any man who was not in position to buy and to pay. We came close together because we both sympathized with the plight of the farmer and we were looking for any opportunity to do anything that promised to help him. We pulled together on that line. That became Legge's ruling passion.

"There was not, I think, another living man as competent as Alex Legge to estimate the damage done France and Belgium by the German armies. The reparations boosters couldn't put a thing over on him. He knew values there both above and below ground and he knew values in Germany, too. He couldn't be pushed into the position of loading on Germany a reparations debt that she couldn't pay. In other words, he refused to be a party to settlement absurdities when the whole civilized world had to be restored to economic balance. Figures in billions of a national debt were just as real to him as those of a small implement dealer's bill for farm machinery. Alex took figures seriously and he would not play ducks and drakes with them to please any diplomat. The French and the English found that out when they drafted the economic sections of the Versailles Treaty. Alex was always looking far ahead to getting the world back on a going basis. His sense of balance in calculations of that kind was astounding."

As general counsel for the War Industries Board, the late Albert C. Ritchie saw much of Alex Legge. Only a few days before the death of Maryland's famous ex-governor, he made this statement to the writer:

"Our minds met on legal problems. His peculiar abilities would be incompletely presented if the fact was not emphasized that no legal counsel could have had more able lay assistance than he gave. I feel certain the lawyers who worked with him in the protracted and involved Harvester litigation felt this. He had the bent of mind that instantly swept aside all unrelated and unessential details and separated them from those facts vital to the legal issue involved. This he did as simply as if by a chemical precipitation. His mental digestion of the facts involved in any problem, legal or otherwise, was amazing and he knew their relation to the issue involved. What a lawyer Alex would have made!"

Clarence M. Woolley was vice chairman of the War Trade Board and liaison man between it and the War Industries Board, by appointment from President Wilson. He was also liaison agent between the Department of Commerce and the War Industries Board.

"One of the greatest compensations of my service as a dollar-a-year man in Washington," says Mr. Woolley, "was an intimate acquaintance with Alex Legge. Mrs. Legge did not make her home in Washington in the war days, but came down only when he indicated that they could have a little time together without interfering with War Industries Board business.

"On hot summer evenings they often took me out with

them to a little Virginia farmhouse where we had the simplest country fare served in true country style. How he did enjoy those meals! Ham and eggs, with home-made relishes, seemed to be his favorite food. After one of these meals, Alex would take me out to a log in the farmyard. Contact with that log seemed to yield him an immediate sense of relaxation and start him telling stories of his early boyhood in Wisconsin and Nebraska, of his youthful business experiences in connection with the operations of the Fuller ranch, of his cowboy days in Wyoming, and his adventures as a collector and salesman for the McCormick Company. Unconsciously in these annals he revealed his passion for farm life and the depth of his attachment for the people of the soil. They were his people. He never outgrew them.

"In my judgment Alex Legge was a master diplomat because he disarmed opposition by his quaint, picturesque, jocular way of presenting his views. He would seize upon the vital principle of a situation and give it a vivid pictorial embodiment that made its point clear. In a sense he was a cartoonist who used words instead of pen or crayon. He could strip a problem right down to the quick in a sentence or a story and leave all his hearers satisfied that his solution was sound. This was an Abraham Lincoln characteristic. He had more of them than any other man I have ever known. To listen to him in an informal discussion was to think of Lincoln.

"Often I have listened to Alex as he talked freely of his thoughts about the World War, the farmers of America and of Europe, and of industrial workers and have said to myself: 'That's the way Abraham Lincoln would have felt and talked.' There was no escape from thinking of Lincoln when with Alex Legge. They were similar in

PRESIDENT HOOVER AND MEMBERS OF FEDERAL FARM BOARD, 1929. SEATED, LEFT TO RIGHT: JAMES C. STONE: SECRETARY OF AGRICULTURE, ARTHUR M. HYDE: MR. HOOVER: ALEXANDER LEGGE (CHAIRMAN); C. C. TEAGUE. STANDING: W. F. SCHILLING; CHARLES S. WILSON; CARL WILLIAMS; C. B. DENMAN. (SAM R. McKELVIE WAS APPOINTED LATER.)—(PHOTOGRAPH BY UNDERWOOD AND UNDERWOOD)

their disregard of all class distinctions, their broad spontaneous human sympathy, their vast gifts of common sense, their logical reasoning powers, and their innate gentleness of heart. Every contact with Legge left me the happier for it."

Very few men who worked with Alex Legge can discuss him without spontaneously comparing his individuality to that of Abraham Lincoln. This similarity is remarked by nearly every one of his surviving associates. It persists almost to the point of monotony, but it cannot be ignored. The volume, character and source of the testimony supporting it forbid. Alex Legge was strikingly Lincolnesque in mind, soul and body. Perhaps no other American has lived since Lincoln who was more so.

Mr. Gerard Swope, now chairman of the General Electric Company, relates:

"I first met Alex Legge in Washington early in 1918 when he was vice chairman of the War Industries Board and I was on the General Staff of the Army, reporting to General Goethals. When General Hugh S. Johnson left Washington to join the troops, General Goethals and I represented the War Department on the War Industries Board. This threw me into constant and intimate contact with Alex.

"No one who knew him at all well ever called him anything but 'Alex' because he was so wholly human. He did not care for titles; he wore no uniform; he dealt fearlessly and frankly with any subject that was brought before him and with anyone whom it involved. The facts of the situation became his sole consideration. And he was quite unembarrassed as to how these facts came to him or who presented them.

"Being human, in the hectic days of 1918 when the

problem of supplying our forces overseas was so tremendously important, he was often worn and therefore impatient; but after the night his contrition was always lovely and sweet—and these words are used advisedly, as they can be for a man as strong as Alex Legge was.

"The only part of any question that remained after he stripped it clean was how we could be of greatest service in expediting supplies to our own forces overseas and to our allies. His mental processes were rapid and he was generous in the recognition of the contributions of others. His fair and frank dealing was based on a fundamental sense of justice, without distinctions.

"In the International Harvester Company, these same ideals and characteristics governed him in the conduct of his business. He considered the public as protectively as he did his stockholders, his employees and his competitors. They all respected him. More than that, they held him in sincere affection."

There is a story behind Mr. Swope's allusion to the fact that Alex Legge sometimes broke under the strain and lost his temper. The incident in Mr. Swope's mind evidently was this:

On one strenuous occasion the almost superhuman patience of Mr. Baruch, under extremely irritating circumstances, sent the vice chairman into a violent eruption.

"Chief," Legge exclaimed, "the prophet Job, at his meekest and lowest, was a rampant old bearcat out looking for blood compared with you. Hell! Haven't you any fight in you? Can't anything make you mad?"

Evidently it could not, for Mr. Baruch took this outbreak with the patient and serene smile that so aggravated his chief lieutenant! The scene was awkward and distressing to all present. But before long Alex Legge was filled with contrition and said, "Chief, I made a damn fool of myself."

To this Mr. Baruch returned the laughing reply: "As usual, Alex! Now forget it."

Steel was perhaps the hottest subject handled in the deliberations of the War Industries Board. J. Leonard Replogle was in command of this and it was his responsibility to protect the accumulation of steel urgently required for war purposes from the assaults of the operators of all non-war home industries using steel. Instead of a "bread line," there was a "steel line" begging for enough to keep their enterprises from starvation and collapse.

"At first," says Mr. Replogle, "these manufacturers seemed utterly unable to comprehend the insatiable demand of the fighting front for steel shells and other war supplies made of steel. Naturally, the automobile industry was in the lead in this fight for enough steel to keep its non-war production going, on at least a starvation basis. It took iron nerve to stand out against these appeals, but in this position I had the unyielding support of Mr. Baruch and Alex Legge.

"Our demand for steel for urgent war purposes stood at 38,000,000 tons. The fate of our own forces at the front and of our Allies depended upon the prompt and steady delivery of munitions and arms. This situation was patiently and repeatedly explained.

"Neither a starving man nor a starving industry is in a state of mind to accept cold reason in the place of sustenance. The guardians of war steel were certainly on the spot and virtually without a friend in the whole camp of home manufacturers who wanted a meager supply of steel for non-war production. Of course the most convincing answer that could be made to these disappointed men was: 'This steel is going to your boys at the fighting front in the form of munitions and arms; a failure in that supply will mean wholesale slaughter, perhaps defeat. In that event you will be without a country.'

"Ultimately, as the war progressed, this reasoning became more understandable to the men in our 'steel line.' At the outset, however, arbitrary and unyielding denial was the only open course and it was followed. Without the unflinching and stalwart support of Mr. Baruch and Alex Legge, my position would have been much more unhappy than it was. This country owes more to those two leaders of the War Industries Board than it will ever realize."

Donald R. McLennan, head of Non-War Construction restrictions on the War Industries Board, declares:

"In forty-two years of business experience, I have never seen such teamwork as we had on the Board. There was absolutely no self-seeking, no pushing for self-advancement, no jockeying for advantages of any sort. Everyone did his utmost and worked harder for a dollar a year than if he were receiving a salary as large as the President's. My job required me to work very late at night. Seldom did an evening pass that Alex did not appear. His passion for work was simply insatiable.

"Those who knew Alex only as a dynamo of executive energy missed acquaintance with his most charming side. He had as great a capacity for sentiment as he had for business. He would do almost anything for a friend—but he suffered keen embarrassment in being thanked for a kind deed. Repeatedly I have seen him walk away under such an ordeal, usually with the remark: 'Oh, go to hell!'"

In the strenuous battles of the War Industries Board, Mr. Baruch found a thrill he had never known as a Wall Street operator. From that day to this, serving his country has been a ruling passion with this man who might naturally have given himself to the enjoyment of a "splendid leisure." And Alex Legge, to the end of his days, was equally unable to resist any nonpolitical call to serve his country. True, he did decline a portfolio in President Hoover's cabinet, but to his mind that post involved politics—an activity for which he felt himself fundamentally disqualified. He had, like Baruch, an impelling sense of patriotism, a willingness to do any hard job that needed to be done for the good of his country in a world that had been plunged into chaos by the greatest war in history.

CHAPTER

XII

At the Paris Peace Table,
1918–1919

T HE first American Foreign Mission on European
soil was that of the War Industries Board, headed
by L. L. Summers. Its twelve members were men
of distinction. Their appointment was due to a misunder-
standing with Great Britain as to prices for war supplies.
President Wilson personally approved of this Mission,
which reached London in the "dog days" of 1918. In
October of that year, Alex Legge, accompanied by Pope
Yeatman and Irvin H. Cornell, was summoned to rein-
force this Mission.

Almost immediately after their arrival the Armistice
was signed. For a few days it seemed that the task of the
War Industries Board Mission was ended. But, owing to
the shrewd vision of Colonel House, it was given a new
and most important job, that of preparing a quick survey
of the devastated territory as to its "industrial status and
requirements." Alex Legge was peculiarly equipped for
this work and threw himself into it with tremendous
energy.

After President Wilson's arrival and early pronouncements, the members of the Foreign Mission became convinced that economic considerations were secondary in his program. So they returned to America, conscious of having provided the future treaty makers with specific and invaluable data on which to adjust reparation claims.

But Alex Legge's return to his business affairs in Chicago was to be of short duration. His willingness to put personal considerations aside when his services were needed by his government was again put to the test.

"Alex Legge never let me down," declares Mr. Baruch. "He was always on call for service to his country. In 1918 he had returned to his duties with the International Harvester Company, happy and contented. But when I cabled him to bring a group of experts to help formulate the economic section of the peace treaty, he dropped everything and came running.

"Those reporting on this mission, besides Mr. Legge, were L. L. Summers, Dr. Frank W. Taussig, Charles H. MacDowell, Frederick K. Nielsen, Bradley W. Palmer, John C. Pennie and J. Bailey Brown. Thomas W. Lamont and I were the American members of the Economic Drafting Section, and Professor Allyn Young, who was independently attached to the Peace Commission, acted as Mr. Lamont's alternate.

"Alex Legge's contribution to this task was of high value. His gift of hard common sense was nothing short of genius. Most of his colleagues on this work were highly educated men. His own academic education had stopped about midway in a country high school course, but he knew the meaning of figures to an extent that was almost uncanny.

"The treaty-makers on the other side were wizards in

diplomacy and economics but Alex was fully capable of meeting them. His mental shortcuts were amazing and his European business experience had given him a specific and comprehensive knowledge of the value of things over there. This was invaluable in connection with reparations estimates."

Baruch says that no country had such a pair as Legge and Summers: Summers with the exact, encyclopedic mind which registered all the facts and the bearing they would have on the subject under discussion; and Legge, the worldly-wise, shrewd Scotch-American who knew how to see that both America and the Allies got justice.

On the Supreme Economic Council, Baruch was Mr. Hoover's alternate. A number of discussions took place in reference to various demands that affected the British interests represented by Lord Robert Cecil who was noted for his integrity and ability. In a disagreement that arose Baruch turned to Legge and asked him for his opinion on the subject under discussion. Lord Cecil interrupted and gave Legge his views and then asked Legge what he thought of them. Legge replied, "This is the God-damnedest nonsense I ever heard." And it was, says Baruch. That ended the discussion and Lord Cecil came to recognize the soundness of the views advanced by Mr. Baruch and Mr. Legge.

The profound impression which he made upon his colleagues in the European Councils following the Armistice is illustrated by the fact that Chandler P. Anderson, the distinguished international lawyer, referred to him as "Legge, the Abraham Lincoln of Industry." This citation was so apt that it stuck to Alex Legge throughout his life.

Any capable American who called on Legge in those days of the European peace adjustments was likely to be drafted for work. Baruch and Legge were discussing who should represent the United States on the Rhineland Commission. Baruch was very anxious to have Legge take the post, but he was overloaded with work and responsibility and was protesting, when in walked Pierrepont B. Noyes, head of the Oneida Community Silver Company, now chairman of the Saratoga Springs Commission and during the War a member of the Price-Fixing Committee of the War Industries Board and connected with the Coal Administration. Legge exclaimed, "Here's your man! Put him on." This was done. Instances of this sort were not unusual.

In the War Industries Board, Charles H. MacDowell, then president of the Armour Fertilizer Works, was director of the Chemicals Division. No diagram is needed to emphasize the tremendously vital part played by chemicals in the great world conflict. Alex Legge and MacDowell were drawn together by many strong ties; they had known each other for years as industrial executives serving the American farmer. As an industrialist, Mr. MacDowell had demonstrated not only his competence as a practical chemical technologist but also as an economist. In their War Industries Board contacts, his ability to deal with broad economic problems inspired the confidence of both Baruch and Legge.

Mr. MacDowell lived with Legge during the latter's entire stay in Paris, worked with him closely on various committees, and was his official alternate on the Committee on Germany. These facts qualify him to say what Legge accomplished in connection with the problems of reparations and economic adjustments which were later incorporated in the Treaty of Versailles. Here is the picture of this great economic enterprise as sketched by Mr. MacDowell:

"The selection of the treaty members was largely made by Colonel House, who picked a remarkable group of university men thoroughly familiar with the various racial elements involved.

"President Wilson was fortunate in having by his side, as economic adviser, Mr. Baruch, who instantly realized that in Wilson's idealistic program for 'making the world safe for democracy' the sordid bread-and-butter matters on the diplomatic table needed to be looked after. Mr. Baruch in turn drafted Alex Legge, so thoroughly Scotch in his thrift and shrewdness, to be his first aid in the economic undertaking before them. This gave Alex Legge the great opportunity of his life to demonstrate his capacity as an international economist and financial diplomat.

"Early in March, 1919, Mr. Legge received a cablegram from Mr. Baruch to come immediately and bring with him a selected group of economic experts to help him in drafting the economic section of the treaty.

"Being daily associated with him in this work permitted me to know Alex Legge, the man, in the highest development of his powers. It is difficult to evaluate the services of any one of the men at the Peace Table. Much of the work was not recorded, and the power of suggestion had a front seat in all of the negotiations leading up to decisions. Alex Legge's work had largely to do with the foundation work on reparations and economic adjustments. He exerted far more influence in these matters than any record could show.

"It was thrilling to watch his transformation from a picturesque American industrialist into an international figure, a world economist whose views on the greatest financial problems ever placed on a diplomatic table were respected and accepted by the keenest minds that the civilized world could command. Beyond doubt, Alex Legge was the most picturesque figure ever present at such a distinguished gathering.

"His reputation along this line had preceded him and was helpful. He remained entirely natural. If he changed in a single particular, it was in an increased modesty, an occasional attitude suggesting something like self-deprecation. This attitude disarmed opposition and encouraged diplomatic opponents to show their hands somewhat unguardedly. But he was utterly regardless of the high rank and great titles of those with whom he dealt. He repeatedly asked such a man, 'Just what is your job, anyhow?'"

It became known at once throughout the highest circles that this tall, awkward, unpretentious man was strikingly "different"—a most interesting novelty. The fact that he had been a cowboy greatly increased his popularity with the sophisticated Europeans. An American cowboy helping to divide the war debts and the economic responsibilities of the great powers of Europe— here was a real spectacle!

Legge became immediately popular with the members of the Supreme Economic Council because of his ready wit and his ability to illustrate his points by homely anecdotes and stories, always apt and amusing. He provided a grateful relief from the strain and formality of ordinarily solemn sessions. Nothing embarrassed Legge and he swiftly pricked one diplomatic balloon after another.

One of the most interesting developments in the field of his personal influence was the increasing demand for his services on the most important committees of arbitration. This was a high recognition of his fairness and vision.

Also it acknowledged the rapidity with which he was able to discharge heavy responsibilities. His action was quick and decisive to a degree that amazed those most concerned in his decisions. He heard all sides to a controversy with painstaking fairness but came to his conclusions with startling dispatch.

Probably there is no better example of Mr. Legge's leadership as an arbitrator than the settlement of what is known as the Mercier or Luxemburg Protocol. It developed that Colonel Mercier, just a month after the Armistice, had negotiated an agreement by which Germany was to supply a specific tonnage of coal or coke in exchange for minette ore from the Lorraine basin. Apparently the representatives of France had neglected to give international notice of this important arrangement, but it was turned up by Alex Legge in his work as chairman of the Committee on Germany.

Under the Mercier agreement, Germany had shipped a large tonnage of coal from the Ruhr, but the minette ore in exchange had not been forthcoming. The French were inclined to be technical because the coal shipments had fallen below the deliveries specified in the agreement. Germany needed food and wanted to pay for it with the coal credit which had been built up, while the French insisted that payments for food must be in gold. The situation called for the ablest sort of arbitration.

"Because I sat with him through the arbitration hearings," relates Mr. MacDowell, "I have definite knowledge of what transpired. It was clearly evident that the Germans had done their utmost to deliver the required tonnage of coal, but had fallen a little short because enough cars were unobtainable. Railroad transportation was in charge of the English stationed at Cologne.

"Alex Legge's brief expedition into Germany just after the signing of the Armistice had given him a definite knowledge of how badly food was needed there. As a leader of the arbitration committee, he worked out a basis of credit for the coal shipments to which Loucheur and his French associates agreed and Germany got the food. Alex put his whole heart into this work because he was so intensely human and kindly.

"Saturday afternoons and Sundays, Alex scoured the devastated regions, his mind sharply focused on the problems of reparations. Often we were accompanied by representatives of the Belgian and Italian governments. In cool weather Alex wore a long overcoat that had seen much service. He made an odd and most informal figure.

"Alex took his only relaxation in the evening, generally reading mystery or detective stories. He never went out socially when he could possibly avoid it."

Legge's methods in his important contacts and negotiations were often decidedly startling, according to Mr. MacDowell, but brought good diplomatic results. His mental faculties were disconcertingly quick—like flashes of lightning. While his decisions appeared to be based on hunches, those who knew him intimately realized that they were the result of reasoning which had outstripped the progress of the statements and arguments to which he was listening.

The main burden of the economic work was borne by the Supreme Economic Council of which Mr. Hoover was the American chairman, with Mr. Baruch as his alternate. In the War Industries Board work, Mr. Hoover and Mr. Legge had been brought into intimate contact. Here Mr. Hoover came to realize the breadth of Legge's powers in dealing with great economic problems.

"My first meeting with Mr. Legge," relates Mr. Hoover, "was during the War when I was United States Food Administrator. Like that of all others who met him, my instant impression of him was of a man having a wealth of common sense, a great business experience, a fine rugged character. I became well acquainted with him during this period from 1917 until the Armistice. Then I went to Europe to represent the American Government in the administration of the Armistice terms and the joint effort of the Allied governments to rehabilitate economic life between the former enemy countries, and incidentally to provide relief. I became the alternating chairman for America of the Supreme Economic Council, the inter-allied body set up for these purposes. Mr. Legge was brought over to Europe for work in connection with the Peace Conference. Frequently I met him in Paris, socially and otherwise. He was a great personality."

Thomas W. Lamont, a partner in the firm of J. P. Morgan & Company, represented the United States Treasury Department on the American Commission to Negotiate Peace, in 1919. Regarding Alex Legge's work in connection with the economic sections of the treaty Mr. Lamont made this significant statement to the writer:

"In that maelstrom of men and events, which was officially known as the negotiations for the Treaty of Peace at Versailles, Alexander Legge stood out with great clarity. He was not a trained economist, yet his mind grasped economic problems with great firmness. He had the knack of separating the elements in a given problem and of properly allocating them. As a great industrialist and as one who was familiar with agriculture on a large scale, he was of immeasurable value in the appraisal of problems having to do with the devastated regions of France and Belgium."

In explanation of his relations with Mr. Legge, Mr. Lamont adds:

"My contacts with him were never closely intimate, and they were at long intervals. Nevertheless, they were such as to make a very deep impression upon me and to make both of us feel that each of us had in the other a real friend. Our first acquaintance came when I went on the Board of the International Harvester Company twenty-five years ago. Then I began to see something of Legge, and these meetings were supplemented by my friendly and semi-official contacts with him at Paris in 1919.

"He was not only highly successful in the management of the Harvester Company, but he commended himself to the entire public by his broad and humanitarian views and his manifest desire to render a real service to the world. He commanded my personal admiration and warm affection."

One incident related by George M. Durkee shows the peculiar dependence of European statesmen upon the information and judgment of Alex Legge. This experience was told by Mr. Legge to Mr. Durkee to illustrate the lack of "common sense" considerations in reporting upon international situations.

Shortly after the war, when he was in London, Legge received a telephone call, asking him to meet several of the leaders of the French Government. They told him they had summoned him because they thought him the "best posted man in the world on European conditions as they actually exist." Then they asked him if he thought the Russians intended to fight France.

Legge said, "No."

"Why?"

"Because they haven't a locomotive up there that could move a train; and if they did have, they haven't a man who could run the locomotive."

And these Frenchmen said, "Well; with all our elaborate reports, that vital point has never yet been mentioned!"

Eugene Meyer, publisher of the *Washington Post*, and former head of the War Finance Corporation and of the Federal Reserve Board, places great emphasis upon Alex Legge's ability to look a long way ahead and illustrates that characteristic by this incident:

"In 1920, when we were still under the spell of war prices, I had a chat with Alex who declared his conviction that we were on the verge of coming out of this trance and getting down to earth. He illustrated the strength of his conviction on the subject by saying that it was up to him to buy a very large quantity of pig iron and the best price he could get was $46 a ton.

"'I told them,' he related, 'that I would not buy at that price or anything like it and that they would shortly wake up to the fact that we were at the threshold of a big break in prices.'

"This doesn't sound very exciting, but it involved a large sum of money. At that time not many business men were awake to the great change just ahead of them. Alex Legge was about the only big industrialist who then saw the price drop that was coming with sufficient clearness to steer his course accordingly. This was one of Alex Legge's strongest characteristics. He saw that the world was not going to stand still, that changes were inevitable and that the operation of economic law was never sus-

MR. LEGGE RECEIVING DISTINGUISHED SERVICE MEDAL FOR WORLD WAR SERVICES, 1923

pended. His perception of impending changes was remarkably acute and dependable. In August, 1921, the
price of pig iron broke to $19.55."

In recognition of his war work, Alex Legge was
awarded the Distinguished Service Medal on June 6,
1923. He also received the decorations of Commander of
the Crown of Belgium, Officer of the Legion of Honor of
France, and Officer Knight of the Crown of Italy.

As His Harvester Colleagues Saw Him,
1919–1929

WHEN Alex Legge returned to private life and to Chicago, he plunged into company affairs as vice president and general manager. The Harvester Company had sustained a loss of many millions in the war period. Its German factory had been long in enemy hands and its French factory had been stripped and was used as a cavalry barracks by the Germans. After the imperial Russian Government collapsed, the Harvester organization faced the fact that every penny it had ever invested in Russia and all its goods and funds there would be lost. This disaster could be weathered only by the most far-sighted management.

Then came the agricultural depression in home territory; wages were reduced, salaries were cut, and factories were put on greatly reduced schedules.

One of the hardest jobs Alex Legge had ever faced was the drastic reduction of the company payroll in 1921 and 1922—an ordeal that was to recur, only with more severity, a decade later. Laying off men was torture to him, but in this dire emergency there was no escape from it.

The problem was to effect the needed economies with the least possible human suffering. This was the vital thing to him. In these payroll amputations the circumstances of every individual employee were taken into account. Long-service employees, men with dependents, men least fitted to stand a siege of unemployment—these were the last to go. Every laid-off employee's address was registered so that he might be recalled when times got better; every effort was made to find another job for every such man; production was carefully "staggered" down in all factories and all branches of the business.

In 1922 Mr. Legge was elected president of the International Harvester Company. Slowly business began to recover and in 1923 prospects became encouraging. Then, in July of that year, the Government reopened the anti-trust suit against the company. Thus, suddenly, an avalanche of the most exacting and responsible work, of a character that could not be delegated, fell upon Mr. Legge.

Again, as had happened in the original anti-trust suit of 1912, Alex Legge was not only the company's most effective witness, but he was a tower of strength to its attorneys in directing the selection, securing and marshaling of witnesses and in the preparation of exhibits to prove that Harvester had lived up to the terms of the 1918 consent decree and that it was guiltless, in purpose or effect, of monopolistic domination in the harvesting machine industry.

As in the earlier case, his was a tremendous task. Counsel in both cases are on record, as are Mr. Legge's fellow executives of that period, in declaring that his energy and insight, his candor and courage and his intimate knowledge of the company's business and of the whole farm implement business were invaluable in helping to win a decision in the supplemental proceeding which, on the Government's appeal, led ultimately to complete vindication of the Harvester Company by the United States Supreme Court.

"It is my personal opinion," says one of the company's attorneys who took part in both cases, "that Alex Legge would have lived years longer if he could have been spared the anxiety and labor involved in meeting these two Government attacks on the company's right to exist. In large part it was his work in assembling and presenting the facts in the case that brought ultimate victory for the company. I have never heard of a case of such magnitude where counsel received more discriminating help from a layman than Mr. Legge gave the company's lawyers in the Harvester anti-trust litigation."

When the trial closed, Mr. Legge was taken seriously ill. His condition failed to improve in Chicago and he decided to try a warmer climate. Engineers of the Harvester Company were doing extensive experimental work with combines in the Imperial Valley, so he determined to go there. Mrs. Legge realized how ill he was and arranged to accompany him.

Mr. H. E. Daniels, then manager of the Los Angeles branch of the Harvester Company, met them at the train at El Centro and was told by Mrs. Legge that her husband was very ill and had run a temperature of 103 all the way from Chicago. He wanted to observe the experiments, but was forced to submit to the arrangements made by Mr. Daniels, who took them to a hotel in El Centro. For ten days Mr. Legge was desperately ill.

Dr. Dayton B. Holcomb, who had been Mr. Legge's physician in Chicago for nearly twenty years, was then living in Pasadena. Mrs. Legge had wired him from

Albuquerque. As soon as possible, they went to Pasadena where Dr. Holcomb secured a bungalow for them. The patient did not improve and was taken to a hospital.

Friends throughout the Harvester organization insisted upon sending physicians and consultants from San Francisco and Chicago, until Dr. Holcomb became almost frantic. He relates:

"During this time the telephone was constantly ringing. Relatives and friends were urgently offering to send specialists. Mr. Legge had made me promise not to let anyone take the authority of his case from me, as he felt that too many opinions were bound to result in confusion. My position was very difficult.

"One day Mrs. Legge told me I was trembling and asked me to talk frankly with her. I told her this was because of the pressure of outside influences, that I was getting wires every day which confused and worried me.

"She talked with Mr. Legge and then asked me to take her to the telegraph office. There she sent a telegram that ended the interference. I think he told her to tender his resignation if they did not leave the case entirely in my hands. Of course these offers of specialists were expressions of great solicitude and it required courage on the part of Mrs. Legge to refuse them so firmly, but she knew her husband's wishes and they were law to her.

"I kept working with Mr. Legge and he finally pulled through. He came in weighing 218 pounds and went out weighing 143, but he walked both ways!"

During this trying period, Mrs. Legge was with her husband continuously. After he left the hospital, she nursed him devotedly. When he became stronger, they spent much time driving about the country and visiting relatives and friends.

They decided to return to Chicago late that summer.

Before leaving, however, they desired to visit their orange ranch just outside of San Diego. On the way down Mrs. Legge became ill, so on their return they stopped at Dr. Holcomb's. He saw at once that Mrs. Legge was quite ill. Privately she said to him, "Yes, doctor, I am ill; but you are worse off than I am. I would rather have you care for me than anyone else, but I am not going to let you assume the responsibility, for I know the strain you have been under during Alex's illness."

Dr. Holcomb gave her the name of a good physician and she was taken to a hospital in Pasadena. He says: "Later I saw that she was steadily sinking. Her doctors said it was typhoid. During my last visit with her, I broke down. She said to me, 'Now you understand why I could not have you. Doctor, I know it is the finish.' "

Mr. Cyrus H. McCormick started for California, but before he arrived, Katherine Legge passed away. That was on August 21, 1924.

The loss of his wife was a devastating blow to Alex Legge. He always blamed himself for her death, believing that her devoted care of him had so reduced her vitality as to render her unable to resist the fever that resulted in her death.

Several Harvester officials were at Rexburg, Idaho, where engineering experiments were being carried on. Mr. A. E. McKinstry, then senior vice president, says:

"Mr. Cyrus H. McCormick decided to stop over there with Mr. Legge on the trip back east, feeling that mingling with some of his old friends might somewhat break the strain of going home. His grief was appalling.

"He had a ranch at Cody which he wanted to inspect, so he and Mr. McCormick and others drove through Yellowstone Park, finally stopping at the Cody ranch.

In the meantime, the rest of us headed for Chicago and arrived there before he did. I met him at the station in Chicago on Labor Day and drove him home for lunch. It was a very sad homecoming."

He had wired Mr. Durkee to meet him at the train at Omaha. "I couldn't believe my eyes!" Mr. Durkee says. "He was the most broken man I ever saw. He was just as intense in his love for his wife as in everything else. He was completely crushed."

Alexander Legge's dream of a beautiful country home with his wife was shattered. He knew he could not live there without her. So he decided to make this estate a memorial to her—a place for rest and recreation for Harvester's women employees and other women workers.

On September 11, 1924, a general office picnic was held at the company's experimental farm near Hinsdale, adjoining the Legge estate. Mr. Legge asked some of the officers and women of the company to meet informally in the living room of the garden cottage and there he told them of his plans for the memorial and asked for suggestions. As a result the Katherine Legge Memorial was granted a charter as a perpetual corporation on October 25, 1924, and trustees were chosen.

Mrs. Legge's ashes were brought from California and on Sunday afternoon, October 18, 1925, a beautiful and impressive service in her memory was held, and her ashes were interred under a boulder of red granite on the gentle eastern slope of the hill. By these services the Katherine Legge Memorial was dedicated to the comfort and happiness of working women, especially Harvester women.

An attractive brick and granite lodge of English architecture, with casement windows and slate roof, was built under Mr. Legge's orders as a clubhouse. A spacious living room with huge fireplace, a restroom, showers and kitchen occupy the first floor. Upstairs is a recreation hall, large enough to accommodate four hundred guests.

The Nettie Fowler McCormick Memorial Cottage, with sleeping accommodations for about fifty persons, was built by Cyrus H. McCormick, Mrs. Anita McCormick Blaine, and Harold F. McCormick and was dedicated June 29, 1929. In 1930 Mr. Legge built the first convalescent cottage and in 1933, Mr. W. M. Gale donated a similar cottage in memory of his wife, who was the first one of the seventeen original incorporators of the Memorial to pass on. Thirty-five additional acres of ground were purchased in 1931 to be added to the original estate. An endowment fund, contributed largely by Mr. Legge, was also provided.

The affairs of the Katherine Legge Memorial are handled by officers and members of the Memorial, and by the Katherine Legge Memorial association.

Picnics and holiday parties are held at the Memorial and week-ends and vacations enjoyed there. A large swimming pool and tennis courts provide for summer recreation. The convalescent cottages are available to working women and their families and a registered nurse is constantly in attendance.

From the moment the Memorial was created, Alex Legge's keenest interests centered there. Every spare hour he could command was spent on the grounds, working with his hands and planning to make this memorial to his adored wife the beautiful place his dreams had pictured.

After his wife's death in California, Alex Legge said he never wanted to visit that state again. But when he received word that his sister, Christina Sharman, was very ill there, he immediately boarded a train for the West and arrived in time to visit with her. On the 29th of July, 1928, she passed away. Her remains were taken to Wisconsin and funeral services were held in the little Methodist church in Montrose to which she had been devoted during her girlhood and early married life, near the old stone schoolhouse where Alex Legge went as a little boy.

Mrs. Carteron, an old friend of the family, says that Alex came to see them after Mrs. Sharman had been buried. "We had some nice old-fashioned flowers in the garden and Alex said, 'I wish you would take some of those flowers up to the cemetery at Montrose. You know, those were the kind Tena liked best.'"

No matter what pressing demands company business made upon him, Alex always found time to visit his relatives and friends in Nebraska, and to stop at the Purple Cane Cemetery where his mother and father rested. Just after the World War, while visiting in the community, he offered to match, dollar for dollar, any sum which the citizens might subscribe toward a perpetual fund for the upkeep of the cemetery. The offer was accepted and the income from this fund has been ample to care for the Purple Cane cemetery.

In 1929 a new parsonage was erected on the church grounds of the Purple Cane community. Mr. Legge left an order with a near-by nursery company to furnish all labor and material necessary to landscape completely the entire grounds.

No one was ever notified beforehand of his family visits. He would turn up at the home of Alex E. Legge, his nephew, and after visiting there for half an hour or so, would go upstairs and get into old clothes. Then he would vanish for the rest of the day, prowling about the farm.

Nephew Alex relates that his uncle had a consuming passion for straightening streams. He says: "One day, in early spring, he and Mr. Durkee, my brother and I were cutting boughs for a dam and floating them down the creek. It was very cold, an early spring snow lay on the ground, and the banks of the stream were extremely slippery. Uncle Alex slipped into the creek. For three hours he worked up to his waist in that icy water and could not be persuaded to change his clothes until it was time to go up to the house for lunch.

"Another time Uncle Alex arrived at the farm during harvest time. We had almost completed shocking 125 acres of oats and had only about an hour's work left. Uncle Alex went out to the field and said, 'You haven't built your shocks right.' He proceeded to demonstrate how they should have been built and we had to go over the whole field and change them.

"One day James was all dressed up in his best clothes when Uncle Alex walked in on one of his surprise visits. He stood talking to James, at the same time giving him the once-over out of the corner of his eye. Finally he reached into his pocket and said, 'Here is some money. Go and get me a pair of overalls—and, while you're at it, get yourself a pair, too.' "

Mr. A. E. McKinstry entered the Deering Company at sixteen and was associated with the International Harvester Company from its formation. He succeeded Mr. Legge as president, retiring in 1935, and is now chairman of the Executive Committee of the Board of Directors.

"I first knew Alex Legge," Mr. McKinstry said, "as a competitor during the days of 'dog-eat-dog' competition among the implement companies. When the consolidation took place, Mr. Legge's job as assistant domestic sales manager was to fuse all those discordant elements. He did a wonderful piece of work in welding that mass of clashing components into a loyal integrated working organization. Irrespective of his official position, his voice was dominant. He forged straight ahead to leadership because responsibility always flows to the individual who can carry it.

"He was utterly honest and he had real courage. Regardless of who composed any group before him or what the situation was, he gave his frank opinion. Those above as well as those below him in the organization felt that if they could get their case to Alex Legge, they would be satisfied with his decision.

"He had a faculty for creating and holding the confidence of people of all classes that was truly remarkable. He was perfectly at home with a group of farmers, of shop employees, or of executives, and he could talk the language of any of the groups with which he found himself. He knew their background and their processes of reasoning and thinking.

"In the early days, large sums of money were borrowed, and Mr. Legge started in to pay back that money. He not only paid it back, but established a reserve fund —a 'kitty' he called it. During those years no one could pry a dime loose from him without a valid reason. Through his wisdom, the company faced its heavy losses during the war and came through in fine shape.

"Mr. Legge was of course greatly interested in European expansion and made many trips to Europe. In

1914, he made one of his numerous trips to Russia. The only way one could get into Russia then was to go up the north shore of the Baltic and around the Gulf of Bothnia to the north end of Finland and climb in the back window and come down through Finland to Moscow. It was the only route open except by way of Vladivostok, which involved a long tedious journey.

"Mr. Legge was called by the imperial authorities to St. Petersburg, where they asked him to sign a contract to make war munitions at our plant at Lubertzy, about twenty miles out of Moscow. He refused. Few men in the world would have stood up against that imperial group in such a way. Mr. Legge said, 'The factory is here. I understand that you gentlemen can compel us to do whatever you wish. If you say we must make these munitions, we will have to, but I will never sign a contract voluntarily agreeing to make them!'

"Years later, following the war and the revolution in Russia, the Soviet government needed our goods—agricultural implements and tractors in particular. We required fifty per cent cash with each order. The profits on these transactions were set aside as a reserve against unpaid balances and finally we got to the point where we never allowed the amount due to exceed this reserve, so that any loss would be taken from this profit, and not from our capital.

"Eventually a big order came along, and they wanted to pay less cash and be allowed longer deferred payments on the balance. We stood firm, but they insisted on seeing Mr. Legge. The Russian spokesman made his plea, saying, 'We have been trading with you over a period of five or six years. Haven't we paid you every dollar we agreed to pay?'

" 'Yes,' responded Alex. 'You have. What's more, you have paid it on time, and we appreciate it highly.'

"The Russian then said, 'Well, if an experience of that kind is not sufficient to establish a basis for credit in commercial transactions, what in the world is?'

"Alex replied: 'Ordinarily that would be true. But we can't forget that you fellows not long ago took everything we had in Russia. We don't know when you might do the same sort of thing again.'

"The argument was over. He maintained our position with reference to the terms."

All those who knew him will agree that Alex Legge had marvelous discernment. In Harvester affairs, the problem of manufacturing to meet the next season's demand is perennial and immensely important. Overproduction is a costly mistake, but so is under-production, involving inability to meet the farmers' demand.

At a certain meeting of the council, consideration of dealer inquiries was the order of the day. A most encouraging volume of dealer inquiries was reported. Mr. Legge listened attentively to the estimates of the number of machines of various sorts that should be manufactured for the coming season. Then he said:

"In the old days, a hundred inquiries reported by a dealer indicated that in a given locality a hundred farmers were definitely in the market for certain machines. Those days have passed. We can't afford to overlook the fact that there has been a big increase in the range of the farmer's riding. He goes places now, and he shops around wherever he goes. In rolling about on rubber, the farmer calls on half a dozen dealers instead of one. This means a big duplication of inquiries."

This observation led to a material scaling down of the

volume of production that had been suggested up to that point. When the sales were in for the year, the wisdom of this course was fully justified. One of his colleagues is said to have remarked, "It took Alex Legge to spot that element in the situation after all the rest of us had let it get past us!"

Nearly every year Mr. Legge managed to make at least two extensive trips over the country. He didn't like to travel alone and usually would take a company man with him. Often he would start at Chicago, going on down to Dallas, returning through Wyoming and Nebraska, and perhaps visiting the Pacific Coast.

He loved to visit with everybody—farmers, merchants and bankers. He could size up situations by these talks. Like a skilled physician with his fingers on a patient's pulse, he could judge from these encounters what the economic situation was going to be for the next six months.

George A. Ranney, now chairman of the Peoples Gas, Light & Coke Company, joined the thirty or forty employees who comprised the general office staff of the McCormick Harvester Company in 1898. When Alex Legge came to Chicago, soon afterward, he at once recognized the abilities of the young man in the cashier's office, and remarked to Cyrus H. McCormick: "There is a man who is going far. We must help him all we can." And as the company grew and expanded, Alex came to rely greatly upon young George Ranney, who rose rapidly to the position of vice president and treasurer of the company.

"When I started to work for the McCormick Company," says Mr. Ranney, "its general office was at Congress Street and Wabash Avenue. Alex Legge came to Chicago during my first year with the company. He was a man of great courage except that he found it difficult to discipline the men who were working under him.

"In the council meetings, when he opposed some move, his favorite address would be: 'Well, I won't agree with that! If you men want to do it, you can—but over my dead body!' One day I said, 'All right. I'll send flowers in the morning. What's the address?' They all laughed— Alex perhaps most heartily of all.

"I visited Alex often when he was in Washington on the War Industries Board, as I happened to be on a committee that was endeavoring to get authorization for supplies of steel and pig iron. He carried a big part of the load down there and did a magnificent piece of work!

"Alex was very practical in his business affairs but this practical viewpoint did not always extend to his human relationships. I was one of the executors of Mr. Legge's estate. From notes and papers found after his death, I know how widely and often how freely he gave help to friends.

"Mr. Legge was habitually frugal in his personal affairs, not stingy. He simply did not know how to spend, but he did know how to invest. Here was the secret of the accumulation of his fortune, considering the fact that, from about 1907, when he became assistant general manager, he received a very substantial salary. When he became general manager, he received what was then regarded as a big salary. His personal and household expenditures were almost unbelievably small.

"The greatest tragedy of Alex Legge's life was the death of his wife. He was devoted to her. One of the most difficult weeks I ever spent was immediately after her death, when I went out to Hinsdale and lived with him."

Mr. T. E. Donnelley, of the famous Chicago printing house, was director of the Pulp and Paper Division of the war organization and in this connection first became acquainted with Alex Legge. This acquaintance was destined to become very intimate, for Mr. Donnelley became and still is a director of the International Harvester Company.

"It is no exaggeration," remarks Mr. Donnelley, "to say that the Harvester organization, from top to bottom, held Alex Legge in an affection that amounted to reverence. As a member for a long period of the Board of Directors of that corporation, I am in a position to understand both the extent of that feeling and the reason for it. His appreciation of loyal and able service and what it deserved at the hands of the company was one of his strongest traits.

"At one session of the Board, the case of a certain man in the foreign service came up. For many years he had given the company faithful service of a value that was hard to overestimate. Then he went to pieces.

"In this meeting the consensus seemed to be that he deserved the severest discipline, that of discharge. Then Alex Legge told us we had no right to do that to an employee who had given the best years of his life to the company and had accomplished invaluable results for it. He admitted that it was, of course, disheartening to see a man of mature years and broad experience 'go haywire' and make a mess of his life. But this, he insisted, furnished no justification for throwing him out when he was most in need of help. The fair and decent thing to do was to go the limit in setting him on his feet again. That would be characteristic International Har-

MR. LEGGE CONGRATULATES CLARENCE GOECKE,
12-YEAR OLD 4-H CLUB WINNER OF GRAND CHAMPIONSHIP
AT INTERNATIONAL LIVESTOCK EXPOSITION, 1928

vester treatment of an employee who had taken a tumble. It was not difficult for Alex to win the disciplinarians to his side.

"The job of setting this man on his feet again was virtually taken over by Alex with the result that he was completely salvaged. He continued his work and eventually was retired and he and his family are now provided for so that they live in comfort.

"While it is true that Alex Legge was strikingly Lincolnesque, I have been deeply impressed with the thought that his mind was singularly like Grant's in its fundamental simplicity. Both of them had a marvelous capacity for hitting upon the most direct solution of a problem without permitting that viewpoint to be confused by complex considerations. No man, I think can read the memoirs of General Grant without a deep appreciation of this quality. Intimate acquaintance with Alex Legge could not fail to reveal the same quality in him. Both of these great men arrived at their conclusions by simple, forthright thinking of a very fundamental sort. They faced the facts of a situation and from them charted their course according to the reckonings of what we call 'plain common sense.'"

Chairman of the Federal Farm Board,

1929–1931

ALEX LEGGE knew when he accepted the chairmanship of the Federal Farm Board in July, 1929, that it would be a thankless task. A day or so after his appointment had been announced from the White House he was in his office in the Harvester building clearing out his desk and getting ready for his new job. Newspaper correspondents and reporters had been hot on his trail for an interview, without success; he simply wouldn't talk for publication.

An alert and persistent young man from the Chicago office of the United Press appealed to one of the Harvester staff. "Mr. Legge has refused to see me," said this young man, "but won't you ask him to give me through you something I can quote—just a few words?"

Mr. Legge listened to this appeal, was silent for a moment and then said, with a characteristic grin: "Well, you might tell him—if you dare—that I know perfectly well I'm going to be the great American goat."

The intermediary was, of course, too wise to relay this message—and what a story the United Press man missed thereby!

Twenty months or more later, after Mr. Legge had given all that he was and all he had to his heroic effort on behalf of agriculture and of the nation's justly balanced economic welfare, there were many other correspondents and reporters seeking interviews with him about many things, including his Farm Board experiences. To all these he had nothing to say.

"I think I have had about enough publicity," he often remarked, "to last any man a long lifetime—most of it, to say the least, highly unfavorable."

When Herbert Hoover became Secretary of Commerce three years after their war work contacts in Europe, he called Alex Legge to come to Washington to advise with him as to the reorganization of the Department of Commerce. Subsequently some sixty to eighty business leaders were brought in and under Mr. Legge's leadership the program for the department was worked out.

In 1922, when the unemployment situation had become particularly acute, President Harding called an Unemployment Conference. Mr. Hoover was the presiding officer and Mr. Legge was again called to Washington to participate.

Mr. Hoover realized the great perception and abilities of Mr. Legge, for he says: "During the entire period when I was Secretary of Commerce, I relied a great deal upon Mr. Legge's advice and co-operation.

"After the election of 1928, I consulted Mr. Legge as to whether he would accept the Cabinet portfolio of Secretary of Commerce but he did not feel that he could leave his business responsibilities. Later, when the Farm Board was created by Congress, and I was faced with the necessity of choosing the Board, a questionnaire was sent out to all farm co-operatives in the United States. Almost unanimously they approved the appointment of Mr. Legge as chairman.

"With this backing, I again sought to draft Mr. Legge into public service. This time, because of his profound interest in agriculture and the endorsement of the farmer representatives, he accepted the assignment for a period of one year. I subsequently persuaded him to stay on longer, but at the end of twenty months, as the Farm Board activities had been organized and his own business responsibilities weighed greatly on his mind, he resigned.

"Six months afterwards, in view of the even greater crisis arising, I endeavored again to bring him into service, but he felt unable to accept.

"Naturally I came to know him with great intimacy. His whole character was one of complete self-reliance. He had learned what every 'rugged individualist' knows: that co-operation and team-work are the essence of progress and that only true individualists are capable of those compromises and co-ordinations which make progress possible.

"He had had a vast and varied personal experience in many parts of the world in contact with all types of men, high and low. He presented exactly the same Alex Legge to every one of them under all circumstances and was just as friendly to one as to the other.

"One of Alex Legge's outstanding characteristics was a desire for friendship, and he won everybody with whom he came in contact except those of whose conduct he disapproved; there he left no indefiniteness of attitude!

"He came to the White House every morning at six-thirty to take part in the medicine ball game played by government officials. At the breakfast which followed, he invariably showed that fine humor which was one of his most lovable attributes, and the day always started a little brighter for Mr. Legge's presence.

"He was not of the type who believed that the world would automatically get better if it were left alone, nor did he have confidence in the future without some human effort to make the machine work. He had great faith in our people and believed that, unless they were defeated by some illusion or demagoguery, national progress would be continuous."

Alexander Legge accepted the chairmanship of the Federal Farm Board because he saw a pioneer's chance to help the farmer help himself. He realized that this was the Government's first major public recognition of the farm problem and believed that, although the Agricultural Marketing Act might not be adequate in its provisions, yet it was the beginning of a movement which promised to raise the level of farm opportunities and conditions to a parity with other industry.

Miss Ina Sharman, Alex Legge's niece, tells of a visit he made at their home in California early in 1929:

"Washington called him on the phone, and he told me they were trying to get him on the Farm Board. 'Hoover is in a hard place with it,' Uncle Alex explained, 'and wants me to help.'

" 'But you are almost worked to death now; and it seems an impossibility to do what they want.'

" 'It is a hard job,' he admitted. 'I hate to get into it, for they can't do what they want to do the way it is set up; but perhaps something can be done.'

"I said, 'The farmers won't stick together.'

" 'They'll have to!' was his answer."

The story of his reluctant acceptance of this post is perhaps best told by Mr. Carl Williams, the cotton member of the Board.

"When I was offered a place on the Federal Farm Board, I refused—not once, but three times! But when I was told by the Chief that he was trying to get Alex Legge to take the chairmanship, I said at once, 'If you get Alex, you can have me, too.'

"Alex Legge and I were interested in much the same subjects and thought alike on many things. In our wanderings over the country we occasionally found friendly fires around which we sat and talked. Those contacts developed a friendship which never wavered.

"I went to Chicago to talk with Alex about the Farm Board. We were familiar with the farm problem and had studied the new Agricultural Marketing Act. After discussing its virtues, defects and possibilities for two days, Alex said, 'Any man would be a damned fool to take a job on that Board!'

" 'I know it,' I said. 'But there have to be a few damned fools in the world in order that the work of the world may get done.'

"Alex's heels swung off the table, his feet came down flat on the floor, and he said: 'Well, I suppose you and I might as well be two of 'em!' He turned to the telephone, called Washington, and talked to the President. The die was then cast for both of us.

"So we two went to Washington, arrived ahead of the other members and spent Sunday at the White House. Out of that first conference came the foundation for the whole national co-operative marketing policy of the Farm Board.

"Alex's keen mind led in all the thinking and planning.

More than once my spirit lagged, but always Alex came along at the psychological moment to say, 'Buck up, Cotton-Top; things might be a damned sight worse, and you're doing fine.' "

On Legge's appointment, a committee of the United States Senate questioned his integrity of purpose, his friendliness for agriculture and the service he could render the farmers of his country. For two days he patiently answered the questions, many of which would have been fitting only in a police court.

Mr. Chris L. Christensen, now dean of the College of Agriculture of the University of Wisconsin, was secretary of the Farm Board during the entire period of Alex Legge's chairmanship. Before this he had been director of the Division of Co-operative Marketing, United States Department of Agriculture.

"Prior to the passing of the Agricultural Marketing Act in June, 1929," he says, "major efforts made by the Government to aid agriculture had been along lines of production. This act was the first big movement by the United States Government to furnish machinery and finances for a program of marketing farm produce.

"American farming is of the commercial type in that the average farmer is producing, not only for his own consumption, but for a market. It is characterized by specialization in certain crops, over large areas of the country. Alex Legge realized that producing is only part of the farmer's job; assembling, preparation for market, processing, warehousing, financing in storage, transportation and distribution to markets and consumers is the other part and is equally important.

"It was Alex Legge's intimate knowledge of farming, together with his broad business experience, that made him an invaluable leader during the first twenty months of the history of the Federal Farm Board when its policies and procedures were inaugurated and the groundwork was laid for making available government funds for loans to co-operative associations."

Mr. Hoover has said: "The most terrible aftermath of all war is its impact on agriculture. War always stimulates agricultural production. War always produces inflation and speculation in farm lands and farm products. Agriculture is much slower to readjust itself than industry. The result is that a long period of disparity between agriculture and industry follows every war. The best example in previous history was the eighteen years of agricultural misery in England following the Napoleonic Wars."

Even during the so-called "prosperous" period from 1924 to 1929, the farmer's income was diminishing. The National Industrial Conference Board report, published in 1926, reached the conclusion that "American agriculture appears to have fallen out of step with the general economic development in the country." Among the reasons given were that farmers lacked national organization to deal with the surplus problem, lacked "organization and system in the marketing processes" that would give them a better return, through adjusting supply to demand in the domestic markets; and also that there was "lack of organization, standardization and grading in marketing," resulting in excessive costs of distribution which could be minimized by "a more systematic contact between producer and consumer."

It was to cope with this situation and to spread to the farmers a share of the prosperity being enjoyed by industry, that the Farm Board was set up.

Alex Legge brought to his task a profound sympathy

for those who were working on the land and a broad knowledge of farm problems. He felt keenly the fact that agriculture was not keeping pace with industry because it was operated as an individual enterprise, competing with highly organized effort in the industries. Industry proceeds on collective action—studied, carefully reviewed again and again by a combination of minds; the farmer acts individually according to his own personal viewpoint.

The problem of agriculture was one of long standing and it was recognized that it could not be solved overnight. The program was to be a long-time constructive one, and would move only as fast as the farmers, through their organizations, were able and willing to accept it.

That Alex Legge believed that the solution of the farmer's problem was to be found in organization is indicated by his remarks before the American Institute of Co-operatives, July 30, 1929:

"All of the Board members, including the chairman, are in complete sympathy with the co-operative movement. . . . The major policy of the Board will be the expansion and strengthening of the co-operative movement."

Again, speaking before the National Association of Farm Equipment Manufacturers in Chicago in October, 1930, he said:

"Collective action . . . is a slow process, an educational movement, and it cannot be done in a few days or months or even a few years."

In an attempt to form a national organization of the then-existing cotton co-operatives, all members were called to a meeting at Memphis in December, 1929. They needed help; but they wanted it in their own way. They argued long and bitterly, relates Carl Williams. At the end of two days of wrangling, Alex Legge "arose in sections" to his full height and said:

"Maybe you'd let me say a few words. This meeting reminds me of the fellow who wanted a well dug between his house and his barn. But the well-driller wandered all over the place working a water switch and announced with great positiveness that the best place was over in the far corner of the quarter section. The farmer said, 'You can gallivant all over the place with that forked hazel switch if you want to, but when you begin to dig that well, you're going to dig right here!' "

The meeting had been tense; but this story sent his hearers into a burst of laughter. There was no more argument and the Farm Board's plan was adopted then and there.

Charles Teague, head of the largest citrus fruit co-operatives in the United States, was called to Washington to offer advice prior to the framing of the Agricultural Act. Soon after its passage, he received a telegram from President Hoover, asking him to serve on the Board representing fruits and vegetables.

Mr. Teague had spent nearly forty years of his life in the co-operative marketing field and was invaluable to Mr. Legge and the other Board members in building up the national co-operative marketing organizations. By the close of the first year, the following national co-operative agencies had been organized: Farmers National Grain Corporation; National Wool Marketing Corporation; American Cotton Co-operative Association; National Livestock Marketing Association; and National Pecan Marketing Association.

"He worked harder than any of us," Mr. Teague says

of Alex Legge. "I often wondered how he stood up under the strain. He was the most untiring worker I have ever known. Alex Legge was of the hardy old pioneer type, frank and sometimes brutal in his statements of things, but full of sympathy and understanding.

"I remember once a co-operative head came to the Board for assistance. He needed $5,000 to keep from being closed out. But his outfit could not legally qualify; the Board could do nothing for him. Mr. Legge loaned him the money out of his own pocket, without security.

"You will find geniuses in all lines of endeavor, but often they are one-sided. Alex had all-round balance. That's rare. He could analyze any situation without losing his perspective.

"I believe that most members of the Board felt that the long-time solution of agriculture's troubles lay in the development of the co-operative movement. Having spent years of my life in co-operative marketing, I have deep faith in the movement. Alex Legge came to realize that there was really no other solution of the problem. The Government can do temporary things in emergencies, but agriculture must be in a position to meet its own problems. The farmer is the most incorrigible individualist in the world. He has always fought his battles alone and is the last to realize the necessity of co-operative action.

"So far as stabilization was concerned, there had never been any attempt to deal with surpluses. When the crash came and everything went down, and the banks were going under, we concluded that we should attempt to retard the down-swing of prices for leading agricultural products so as to avert a general panic. We did retard the downward trend for some time; had we not done that, you would have had a wholesale failure of banks through the great Middle West."

When the Agricultural Marketing Act was passed by the House of Representatives, after a decade of Congressional consideration, it contained no provisions for stabilization of the price of commodities. The act had been originally outlined by President Coolidge and its essential features were formulated in 1927. Not until the bills were in conference, in 1929, were provisions introduced authorizing the Farm Board to recognize stabilizing corporations covering those commodities which required such organizations in preventing and controlling surpluses so as to avoid undue depressions in prices. It had been difficult to secure the legislation, and as it was not believed that any situation would arise where such use of these powers would be involved, President Hoover, rather than destroy the work of many months of Congress, signed the bill.

That Alex Legge believed that the Farm Board would never be called upon to exercise the stabilizing powers of the Agricultural Marketing Act is shown by his statement of July 30, 1929, before the American Institute of Co-operatives in Baton Rouge, La.: "The Federal Farm Board, as now organized, is not going to buy or sell any commodity, agricultural or otherwise."

At the time of the stock market crash, the crop of 1929, produced at a very high cost to the farmer, was in process of being marketed, the majority of the crops being directly or indirectly on the farmers' hands or hypothecated for loans from country banks and merchants.

When the market collapsed, a panic started in the commodity markets which threatened to bring immediate ruin not only to the farmers but to all who had advanced money to the farmers. The situation resulting from the dumping of agricultural products the moment they had passed below the margins upon which loans had been made would have brought wholesale catastrophe had not the Farm Board gone into stabilization activities. These operations would have been more successful but for three years of bumper crops and a resultant surplus of unusual dimensions at a time when the world consumption was also falling.

Correspondence between Chairman Legge and President Hoover clearly indicates that both men viewed stabilization as a measure to be used only in case of emergency.

In his letter to President Hoover dated March 6, 1930, Alex Legge said:

The major duty of this Board as we see it is to develop and strengthen co-operative associations, and advance loans to them to the end of building up substantial farmer-owned and farmer-controlled organizations for each of the major agricultural industries, which in turn can bring greater stability to the agricultural markets. Considerable progress had been made in laying the foundation for such organizations when our plans were seriously interrupted and the work made increasingly burdensome by the crash in the security market last fall, followed as it was by the tendency for serious depression in commodity prices.

Since this occurred, our work has of necessity been largely of an emergency nature, not only because of immediate importance but because of the fundamental necessity of trying out methods by which the farmer may be protected from forces of instability for which he is not responsible.

The collapse of the stock market was checked by groups of bankers and commercial interests stepping into the breach and providing large sums of money, perhaps in the aggregate approximating the $500,000,000 authorized by Congress in the Agricultural Marketing Act. We have seen no indication of similar action on the part of banking and commercial interests on commodity prices, although it is rather generally conceded that the interests of the public are more involved in commodity prices than in security prices. Perhaps the financial and business interests feel that the action of Congress in passing the Agricultural Marketing Act made it the job of this Board to deal with an emergency such as now exists. . . .

Stabilization seems to be generally regarded by the public as an attempt to raise or fix prices. This is not correct. Effective stabilization should prevent excessively high prices as well as extremely low prices, and the elimination of these fluctuations would be in the interest of processors and consumers as well as producers and could affect adversely only the element of speculation. . . .

The Board's connection with the matter is the furnishing of credit to farmers' organizations and the stabilization corporation which they have set up. As time goes on and they become better organized, they should be, and we believe will be, able to conduct such operations without government aid or interference. . . .

President Hoover's answer, dated March 15, 1930, contains these statements:

The major purpose of the Board, as you say, is to build up farmer-owned, farmer-controlled marketing organizations under the other sections of the act. This will require years of steady building toward a reorganized marketing system, but without this foundation I see no permanent realization of our hopes of a new day for agriculture. In any event it has been my view that "stabilization" in any form was absolutely dependent upon building up competent farmer-owned and farmer-controlled marketing organizations in the different commodities to a point where they are in position to provide, first, stability through orderly marketing and elimination of waste; second, to accumulate sufficient capital to constitute a real equity under loans made by the Board; and third, to assure storage and other marketing facilities—and above all, to be equipped with competent and experienced staffs so as to conduct their business without interference and detailed direction from the Board. . . .

I am glad to know from you that the operation (stabilization) has so far been successful in stemming a panic and slowing the fall in prices so that the grain farmer has realized prices much above the point he would otherwise have secured and has thus saved many hundreds of millions directly and indirectly to them and contributed to re-establish stability in business in general. It is of course too early to see the final results of this action. The difficulties and dangers to the farmer which have already developed in it are indeed an indication that nothing but a most unusual emergency warrants its use. Whatever the results are, it will have compensations in experience.

But I am concerned with the necessity of drawing for the future a complete defined separation of the government from stabilization activities, and the building of a sound system of independent farmer marketing institutions through other powers of the Board.

In 1935, Mr. Hoover dictated this statement: "The operations of the Farm Board can be considered as a part of the general policies of the Administration to cushion the collapse which came from the crash due to the orgy of speculation and the collapse of the European financial structure eighteen months afterwards. . . . The European financial panic resulted in destruction of currencies, repudiation of debts; and one phenomenon was the attempt of nearly all European powers to limit imports with a view to producing favorable balances of exchange. Quotas on wheat and cotton, higher tariffs, and other devices were applied—all of which tended to limit the market for American agricultural products."

Only ten per cent of the Board's time and half of its funds were used in stabilization activities; ninety per cent of its time was used in organizing and assisting co-operatives.

Sam R. McKelvie, the grain member of the Board, ex-governor of Nebraska and a close personal friend of Alexander Legge, relates how the Board was drawn into the purchasing of wheat:

"The 1929 crop was extremely heavy. Prices were not inviting for export. As the southern terminals were filled to overflowing, wheat began to move northward. The Kansas crop came in and, finding a part of its space pre-empted, moved up the river to Omaha and even to the Twin Cities. Nebraska's crop arrived and found the terminals full. Trainloads of wheat stood on the tracks.

"By early October, the demands upon the Board for action were insistent. What was the Board good for if it could not halt a price debacle like this? Talk about organizing co-operatives so that farmers might control their marketing was all very well, but it was too intangible; it did not meet the existing emergency. Telegrams rolled in: 'Set up stabilization operations at once!' 'Buy wheat!' The most insistent of these came from the large speculators, with farm leaders joining heartily in the chorus.

"On that fateful day, October 20, 1929, as the securities markets went into a nose dive, the commodity markets settled into a tail spin. It became imperative to do something quickly for both wheat and cotton. Buy what? Not government buying—no sir! That was out from the beginning. Nothing would be condoned that savored of government-in-business or price-fixing.

"So it was decided that the loans should be made through the existing sectional or regional co-operatives—the national co-operatives had not been set up. Following an all day meeting in Chicago, the newspapers flared forth that the Farm Board would spend 'a hundred million dollars' and even more if necessary, to save the wheat farmers from the baneful effects of the stock market collapse. That did the trick: the market steadied.

"It soon developed, however, that these loans were a mere stopgap against the time when more significant things must be done. But it did give the Board a breathing spell while it proceeded with the organization of national co-operative sales agencies for grain, wool, cotton and livestock.

"The new national co-operatives were born none too soon. By this time the edge had begun to wear off the

KATHERINE LEGGE, WIFE OF ALEXANDER,
FROM AN OIL PORTRAIT BY JEF LEEMPOELS, BRUSSELS

loans. In December prices began to slip again. The setting up of stabilization operations under Section 9a was the only alternative. In early February, 1930, the Grain Stabilization Corporation was formed to buy wheat.

"It was by this arduous route that the Farm Board finally went the whole length in buying wheat, and it took every step reluctantly. The telegrams that came across Washington desks during these transitions would have curled the hair of a much more case-hardened citizen than Alex Legge or any of his colleagues. The 'injured interests' made the going as tough as possible. When the Board began buying wheat for future delivery it was charged with speculation, and to this day that charge is uttered by those who know how untrue it is. It was in reality supporting the market by every legitimate means possible. And it did help. Farmers were enabled to get substantially better prices than they otherwise would have received at the time.

"When the new crop began to come in, prices continued to decline. In addition to the farmer's plight, a Congressional election was at hand. Day after day the doorway of the Board chairman was darkened by the haunting figures of Congressmen, Senators, and other government officials, demanding that the Stabilization Corporation buy wheat.

"Then a devastating drouth swept across the southeastern states. It was quite evident that millions of people and thousands of cattle would have to be fed by unusual means. Without any public announcement of it, the Farm Board authorized the purchase of wheat, barley and oats for drouth relief purposes. The quantities secured were not large but, judiciously purchased on the low spots of the market, they helped substantially to bolster up prices.

"Throughout the Congressional election, the Board stood aloof from political influence; and all the time it was supporting the market with the drouth relief purchases. Had this been known, not a few Republican Congressmen in wheat territory who went down to defeat might have been saved. But Alex would not let it be said that the Board had been used to promote the political fortunes of anyone.

"Shortly after Thanksgiving the real price debacle came; drouth relief purchases would no longer suffice. The Grain Stabilization Corporation resumed buying and from that time until the new crop came in, seven months later, the market in this country was maintained at an average of about 25c above Winnipeg.

"The benefits that resulted from this can hardly be measured. Numerous bank failures were averted; farmers were enabled to market their wheat at a fifty per cent premium when and as they needed the money; millers were accommodated in getting the kinds of wheat they wanted with the minimum of inconvenience; congestion was prevented at the interior terminals when the next crop came in; and the loss was not borne by the farmers.

"I have known a lot of men—eminent men—but none have I known that impressed me as being so outstanding in their own right as Alex Legge. It was with the utmost reluctance that Mr. Legge accepted a place on the Farm Board, but having once undertaken the task, no work was too great. Night after night he left the office carrying a portfolio filled with mail he had not had time to read during the day. He read carefully every worth-while thing that came across his desk. He had a rare capacity for sifting the wheat from the chaff and his memory of the things he read was marvelous.

"He worked for neither pay nor glory but only to get the job done in a creditable way. He was without partisanship—so much so that if it appeared that an appointment under the Board was being made for that reason, he vetoed it. The costs of government stirred his ire and he stormed at the bureaucrats who were incessant in their extravagances.

"Among those of us who worked with him, there is the conviction that the tremendous load he carried then went far toward shortening his days."

George S. Milnor, who became president of the Grain Stabilization Corporation a month after its organization, comments thus upon the activities of this corporation:

"Up to the time the Grain Stabilization Corporation was established, some 20,000,000 bushels of wheat had been purchased through existing co-operative associations and ordered to storage in various markets. The pressure of wheat on the market continued to increase, however, and contracts for future delivery were declining to such an extent that grain men and millers throughout the country were protesting vigorously.

"The Administration and the Farm Board realized the difficulties and criticism that would be encountered if they extended their operations to cover the purchase of contracts for future delivery. After much deliberation and with reluctance, they decided to enter the futures market in a small way, hoping that the combined buying of cash wheat and futures would stem the decline which was threatened in view of the constantly increasing surplus during the previous few years. The market rose rapidly.

"It soon became evident, however, that the speculating public not only was inclined to construe the activity as an effort to stem the decline, but also felt that the result would probably prevent any material upturn in prices and that therefore little was to be gained by continuing to buy wheat futures. As speculators withdrew from the market, it became necessary for the Stabilization Corporation to buy such released holdings in addition to hedges that were placed by millers and others who had accumulated stocks of cash wheat.

"In the light of evidence recently disclosed at hearings conducted under the authority of the Grain Futures Act, it now appears that it was necessary for the Stabilization Corporation not only to absorb the hedges that had formerly been carried by the speculating public, but also to buy the millions of bushels of short wheat that the large speculators continued to dump on the market.

"By the end of the crop year, June 30, 1930, the total amount of wheat owned by the Stabilization Corporation was 66,000,000 bushels. This wheat was all paid for and stored in various locations, mostly in terminal markets throughout the country. The Farm Board announced that the Stabilization Corporation would not sell its accumulated holdings during the harvest movement and it is a fact that during the heavy harvest movement of June and July, 1930, there was less congestion in terminal markets and at Gulf ports than in the previous year, and prices prevailing in such markets were much higher compared to the world levels than during the preceding year before stabilization operations were started.

"The purchase of wheat for use in the southeastern territory, then suffering from severe drouth, helped the market materially but not permanently. Co-operative associations and individuals who had stored their new crop and borrowed money on it in order to avoid placing it on an unwilling market, were faced with foreclosure sales, which in turn would have dumped millions of bushels of wheat on a market totally unprepared to receive it. Large purchases were made by the Stabilization Corporation and a definite minimum price of 81c a bushel was established in Chicago for May 1931 contract—a very fair price compared with wheat values in other countries and in view of prevailing economic conditions.

"Opposition to the stabilization effort was rampant, in spite of the fact that stabilization buying gave all owners of wheat, including farmers, grain dealers and millers, an opportunity to dispose of their surplus at the 81c basic price. Without such buying there is little doubt that the price of wheat would have declined to 45c a bushel, Chicago, and the producers and holders of wheat would have been forced to sell at prices which would have netted them many millions of dollars less than they actually did receive.

"On December 31, 1934, the Grain Stabilization Corporation had returned to the 'revolving fund' all but $75,886,970. But it had due it from the German and Chinese governments and other solvent debtors $10,-203,194, leaving the operating loss at $65,683,786. In round numbers, the cost of maintaining the price of wheat over the entire country throughout two years of enormous production was less than $66,000,000—and this when world wheat prices had declined far below that price level.

"Compare this with the $98,223,175 paid our wheat growers for the fiscal year ending June 30, 1935, by the A.A.A. to curtail production over a period of severe drouth and poor crops during which the price remained below 85c a bushel. That $98,000,000 came direct from consumers of wheat products, of whom the 'poor' enormously outnumbered the 'rich.' The $66,000,000 deficit of the Grain Stabilization Corporation came from the United States Treasury, from those prosperous enough to pay income and excise taxes. These stabilization operations resulted in the handling of more than one billion dollars worth of the largest surplus stock of wheat our country ever had."

As chairman of the Farm Board, Alex Legge bore the brunt of the widespread and skilfully propagandized criticism of this venture. Abnormal conditions forced the Board into market operations of a kind that normally would not have been attempted. The measures were designed to meet an emergency. Certainly that emergency did exist, and certainly it was met.

If he was sometimes hurt by this criticism, he gave no indication of it. He was interested solely in the thing to be done and in the result of his efforts, without thought of himself or what people were going to say or think about it. If he was convinced that he was doing the right thing, he would go ahead and do it.

While Alex Legge did not often reply to his critics, there can be no question but what he was very much aware of their attitude. Several months after his resignation, he visited Washington and ran into a Congressman who had been one of his bitterest critics. The Congressman beamed on him and asked him to lunch. Legge drawled: "The last time I saw you, the only reason you didn't tar and feather me was because you didn't have either the tar or the nerve."

Alex Legge's sense of humor was unquenchable. His

experience on the Farm Board did not make him bitter. Some months later, as he and Sam McKelvie were riding around the capitol at Lincoln, Legge teased McKelvie about his being the "wheat man" on the Board, working to curtail production, and then having a statue on top of the capitol building of a man sowing wheat.

In his efforts to convince the farmers that curtailment of production was necessary, Mr. Legge, with other members of the Board, made repeated tours through the agricultural districts, speaking day after day to farmer groups. He knew the job was one of slow education. An amusing incident relating to these efforts in crop reduction is told by Carl R. Gray, president of the Union Pacific System:

"Mr. Legge and I were on a committee appointed by Senator Capper to determine the recipient, each year, of an appropriate gold medal and $5,000 in cash for 'distinguished service to agriculture.' Among others, we were considering a scientist who after many years of service was being retired by the United States Department of Agriculture. One of his many accomplishments in entomology was a plan for overcoming the chinch bug.

"Mr. Legge, then chairman of the Federal Farm Board, was struggling with the question of crop control. He leaned over to me and said: 'Hell, I can't vote for this bird; what I want just now is more chinch bugs.' Nevertheless he joined the rest of us in making this deserved award."

C. B. Denman, representing livestock on the Board, says that during the unusual heat of the first summer in Washington, Mr. Legge never lost his good humor and patience.

"It was during these days that a man appeared before

the Board who felt that he must make an impression by using many Latin expressions. After Mr. Legge and the other members of the Board had listened attentively for some time, Alex said in an aside to another member, 'Is this fellow trying to say mass?' Then he quietly turned to the man and said, 'Now if you will talk plain English which we farmers can understand, we will get right down to a study of your problem.'

"The Farm Board members, together with several other government officials, were guests of President and Mrs. Hoover over the Labor Day holiday at Rapidan Camp. The President suggested that we build some trout dams in the Rapidan. Mr. Legge immediately organized the forces and assigned each of us a job; to Secretary of Agriculture Arthur Hyde and Secretary Newton, he allotted the work of pulling up thousand-pound boulders with ropes, directing them as he would have a yoke of oxen. One or two were conscientious objectors, but needless to say, the trout dams were built, despite the fact that the work almost put some members in the hospital to recuperate from working waist-deep in a cold mountain stream trying to come up to the expectations of the muscular chairman of the Farm Board.

"As time went on and our work on the Board progressed, the thing that struck me most forcibly was Mr. Legge's ability to measure a man and his motives. Sometimes, when he thought a man was not sincere, he would appear to go to sleep reclining in his chair with his feet on the table, but I soon came to know that he was not missing a single word. Once when a man had talked about thirty minutes and then struck the table and said, 'Now I am coming to the point,' Mr. Legge's feet came

down off the table and he exclaimed: 'Good! I was wondering if there was one.'

"A session of the Board was seldom held that he did
not amuse us with his Lincolnesque diplomacy and good
humor. He could and did violently oppose his friends,
but only to draw out their reasons for opposition and
test their strength of character in standing up for their
convictions.

"A friend who knew that he sometimes used rather
incandescent language in arguing matters with his colleagues once asked, 'Why don't you reply to some of your
critics that way?'

"Mr. Legge's answer was: 'I sometimes lose my temper among my friends—never among my enemies.'

"The activities of those who opposed the Board were
taken as a matter of course by Mr. Legge and did not
trouble him greatly, but he was disappointed that the
farmers, who could have benefited, did not co-operate
more generally.

"Once Mr. Legge clashed with a good friend because
he thought this man was recommending what to him
seemed a raid upon the Treasury for millions of dollars.
He was uncompromising when he thought anyone was
attempting such a move, and his language was so em-
phatic that it was taken as a personal affront. This man
came to me later white with anger and asked what he
should do. I told him to go directly to Mr. Legge and
tell him how he felt.

"When he told Mr. Legge he had been misunder-
stood and was hurt and offended, Alex was instantly con-
trite and said: 'You are exactly right and I can only ask
you to forgive me.' Mr. Legge would go any length to

heal a wound that his words or actions had caused, but he was uncompromising when he thought a thing was morally or legally wrong."

There were endless engagements to make speeches at banquets and dinners, conferences and conventions, reports to Congressional committees, and broadcasts over the radio networks. Mr. Legge fulfilled these demands convincingly; his sincerity carried conviction. He could talk to thousands as well and as easily as to one; he entirely lacked egotism, but he had no inferiority complex.

He had little time or inclination for social affairs. Mr. McKelvie tells this story:

"When Premier Ramsay MacDonald visited the President, Washington society was on its toes. A bid to the dinner that was to be given him at the White House was prized above all else. Alex received one. That day, as we were returning to Washington from Chicago, he bewailed the invitation; to go would knock him out of 'a whole evening's work.' I expressed my regret that the invitation was not transferable, as I would gladly go. When I went to the office that evening, there was the chairman!

" 'Not going to the party for the Premier?' I asked.

" 'No; I called the Chief up and he let me off.' "

At the White House it is the rule that guests may leave only after the President has announced: "Gentlemen, we will say good night." One evening, about nine-thirty, Mr. Legge, tired and yawning, turned to President Hoover and said, "Mr. President, I am tired and sleepy. Don't you think you ought to get some rest?"

President Hoover chuckled and said, "Well, gentlemen, we will say good night."

Carl Williams tells of an incident following the receipt of a dinner invitation by Mr. Legge.

"One night Alex was invited to a dinner by Eugene Meyer, then chairman of the Federal Reserve Board. Dinner was to be at eight. Alex's concession to Gene Meyer was a clean shirt and collar, a fresh tie and a change from one business suit to another. I drove him to Meyer's house on Crescent Place, on my own way home to dinner, and dropped him at the door at exactly seven-thirty.

"The next morning, I asked, 'Well, Alex, was Gene home when you got there?'

"He grinned, rather sheepishly, and confessed: 'I didn't go in until eight o'clock. I walked around the block six times.'

"'What for?' I asked, astonished.

"'Well, dinner wasn't till eight.'

"'What of it?' I asked, still more puzzled. 'Did you think Gene would bite you or something?'

"'Hell!' he said, 'I'm not afraid of Gene Meyer; but I'll be damned if I was going to face that perfect butler of his a half hour ahead of time.'"

But the story which perhaps more than any other delighted the press correspondents at Washington was this:

During the celebrated controversy between Mrs. Longworth and the sister of Vice President Curtis as to which should take precedence at formal dinners, a reporter asked Alex Legge where he thought the members of the Farm Board should be placed.

Mr. Legge's reply came quick as a flash: "Hell, we're farm hands. We'll eat in the kitchen with the other help."

His niece, Miss Ina Sharman, felt that his Farm Board experience had broken him physically.

"When he came back," she said, "I noticed that Uncle Alex had become bent. He said he thought he had worked for the International Harvester Company, but he never knew what work was till he went to Washington on the Farm Board. When I remarked that he had at least got back alive, he said, 'Oh, they really used me very nicely. I have no complaints whatever. It was hard work, of course!'

"One of our friends wrote me during his stay in Washington: 'You never say anything to show that you are proud of the honor he has had and the work he is doing. We are all so proud of him.'

"I answered: 'I think it will kill him before the year is up. How can I be glad?' And yet I was proud of his willingness to try to help others."

In the letter to President Hoover which accompanied his resignation from the Farm Board on March 5, 1931, Alex Legge said:

While the work of the Board is only started, yet the organization work on which I promised to assist has progressed to a point where this agency might be justly classified as a going concern. . . .

Perhaps the most difficult problem we have had to deal with has been the belief on the part of so many of the farmers that the government could, through some magic process, bring about prosperity for them without any action on their part. Substantial progress is being made in convincing those whom the Board was created to serve, that lasting results are dependent upon their own actions rather than on anything others can do for them, and that the process of putting agriculture on an equality with other industries depends largely upon their adopting the same basic principles which have resulted in a greater measure of prosperity to others. . . .

While there are still a few of the agricultural leaders who lower their voices when they speak of production control, yet practically all of them have accepted the principle as essential.

A world-wide depression, perhaps the worst one in history, has made progress seem slow, but it is my judgment that we are building on a better foundation for the future than would have been the case under more favorable conditions. Experience to date convinces me that more permanent lasting benefits to the agricultural class can be accomplished under the provisions of the Act than I believed possible at the time the work was undertaken.

In leaving, I wish to say a word of sincere appreciation for the earnest, untiring efforts of my associates on the Board. Action taken has not been that of an individual, but has reflected the thought of the Board as a whole. Decisions have been unanimous on all important questions of policy and practically so on each individual transaction.

In my judgment the change in the chairmanship will prove beneficial and the progress of the work will soon convince even the most skeptical that the Board is a permanent, useful and helpful institution, not an experiment as it is so often referred to by those who frequently criticize its operations.

President Hoover, in accepting the resignation of Mr. Legge, wrote:

The many times I have urged that you remain as chairman of the Federal Farm Board are perhaps, in themselves, an indication of my feeling about your resignation. Through this service you have added another notable contribution to the agricultural industry and to the country at large.

If I thought it would be of any avail, I would even at this late date urge you to remain in the service. I know the sacrifices you have made in undertaking it, and I am sure if you could conscientiously do so, you would continue. I am in hopes that matters may be clarified so that you can again enter public service at a later date.

The knowledge that James C. Stone, the tobacco member of the Board, and its vice chairman, would succeed him as chairman gave Alex Legge solid assurance that the work would be continued along the lines and policies already established. Their understanding of each other was rare and fundamental. Their minds clicked on the basic things involved. Legge knew that Stone would hold fast and follow the course they had charted together; that the Kentuckian was devotedly loyal to the farmers and understood their problems as he himself understood them. They saw eye to eye the dangers which threatened the co-operative movement.

After Mr. Stone succeeded to the chairmanship he frequently consulted Mr. Legge on puzzling problems and was always given co-operation. Confidence and affection were a continuing bond between them.

XV

Back Again to Private Life and Business, *1931–1933*

ALEXANDER LEGGE left his heavy labors on the Farm Board with a weariness which he could not conceal, but his chin was still up. He was tired, exhausted, but not defeated.

No man in the country had a clearer understanding than he of the financial catastrophe which would have swept the agricultural states had not the Farm Board and its agencies supported agricultural prices when all the forces of nature, economic circumstances and speculative greed conspired to plunge them to abysmal and unprecedented depths. This was a victory that would be recognized later. Lack of appreciation and applause was the least of his worries. He was singularly callous to public opinion as long as his own conscience and convictions approved his course. "A tough hide!" was his self description.

The stock farmers of his own Eastern Nebraska were hard pressed for operating funds when he retired from the Farm Board and returned to the Harvester Company. Government agencies for making loans on livestock had not then been generally developed. Cattle men in urgent need of funds were forced to depend upon loans from local banks. These were so tightly restricted as to be virtually unobtainable. Farmers who had long been good credit risks at banks at which they had done business for years were daily denied loans.

Realizing their unhappy situation, Mr. Legge wanted to do something to help tide them over. The Folda bank in Schuyler was surprised to receive from him a check for $10,000 with instructions that it should be loaned to the smaller cattle growers of that community, with as wide a distribution of the money as possible. He explained to Mr. Jarslov Folda that this was his own private money and he was sending it simply because he wished to give "the little fellows" in the cattle business in his home community a helpful boost. The interest rate to be required on these loans was low. At the same time, he sent his check to Mr. E. F. Folda, in Omaha, for $100,000 with similar instructions. This characteristic act is the best possible proof that Alex Legge's heart was still with the farmers.

In this general period many pleasant recognitions came to Mr. Legge in proof of the fact that economists at home and abroad regarded him as having a better understanding of farm commodities and their markets and of farmers and their problems than almost any other man in the country.

For twenty-five years it has been the annual practice of the College of Agriculture of the University of Wisconsin to accord honorary recognition to four or five farm leaders for distinguished service to agriculture and rural life on the occasion of the institution's annual Farm and Home Week on the campus at Madison. On February 1,

MAIN BUILDING OF KATHERINE LEGGE MEMORIAL, HINSDALE, ILLINOIS

1932, Mr. Legge was one of five given this honorary recognition. Dean Chris L. Christensen of the College of Agriculture bestowed this distinction upon Mr. Legge "as one who knows the problems of farming, who has proved his worth and his unselfishness in an effort to serve American farmers and farming."

In 1932 Mr. Legge served as a member of the National Transportation Committee, under Ex-President Calvin Coolidge as chairman and Bernard M. Baruch, vice chairman. Also serving on this committee were Ex-Governor Alfred E. Smith and Clark Howell. Dr. Harold G. Moulton, of the Brookings Institution, headed the research staff. Regarding this important undertaking, Ex-Governor Smith relates:

"At the request of a number of life insurance companies and savings banks in the City of New York, in 1931 I consented to serve on an unofficial commission to make a study of the financial structure of the railroads of the United States.

"Mr. Legge took a very deep interest in this matter. Although he had to travel from Chicago to attend the meetings and hearings, he never missed one. He brought to the executive meetings of the commission a fund of knowledge acquired in his long business experience. He was quick to grasp every situation brought out by the testimony in the public hearings. His was a very intelligent contribution to the report that finally came from the commission. It was his good, hard common sense that made him so useful in this work. He seemed to get at every point rapidly and lost no time discussing subjects that were not germane to what was before us. He was the typical hard-headed, horse-sensed business man.

"In addition to his business sagacity and his high order

of intelligence, he was a most companionable man. I enjoyed working with him and felt I had made a very valuable addition to the circle of my good friends."

The comprehensive report of this committee is one of the most searching surveys of transportation in America in existence. It is a basic document which commands the highest respect from all who deal in a practical way with the railroad problem in this country. The conclusions of the committee start with the statement that: "The railroad system must be preserved. . . . Government policies should be freed of any purpose either to favor or to handicap any form of transportation with relation to any other form. . . . Regulation should not attempt to 'run the business' of transportation. It should concentrate on protecting the public against discrimination and extortion and on requiring the most efficient service at the lowest competitive cost."

The independent, nongovernmental character of this investigation, the high ability of the members of the committee and the fact that it was brought about by the great insurance companies and savings banks carrying a vast volume of railroad securities give the report of this committee a peculiar authority and value.

That the whole course of Alex Legge's life was profoundly changed by the death of his wife is known to all of his intimates. Why he devoted himself so intensively to the Harvester business is revealed by a remark he made to Mr. Cowan: "Henry, I don't give a damn for money. Since Mrs. Legge passed away this business has become everything to me. It is my chief interest in life. It keeps me going."

He made frequent trips to Europe and in 1927 he toured South America, investigating the great farm areas of Brazil and the Argentine. In 1932 he spent months studying farm problems in England, France, Germany, Denmark and Sweden. He drove himself to constant activity and disliked to be alone. He entertained at his Hinsdale home constantly. The men who were associated with him in Washington, as well as Harvester men from out of town, made a special point of visiting his home whenever they came to Chicago. On holidays, however, he persistently avoided human companionship. They were very tenderly associated with Mrs. Legge, who had made them times of peculiar gaiety and delight. If possible, after she had gone, he would spend the holidays on shipboard. To old friends who invited him to Christmas and New Year celebrations he would reply that he would "try to make it"—but he took good care to be alone on board some ship on these occasions.

Carl Williams, in whose home he was a frequent guest, relates: "Once, when we were at Hinsdale, Alex told us the story of the happiness of his married life, of how he and Katherine planned the home that was never built, and of the Katherine Legge Memorial which took its place. My wife frankly wept—and I wanted to. That intimate confession was a wonderful revelation of the real Alex Legge. He never referred to the subject again."

One friend who took advantage of every possible opportunity to visit the Legge estate was Herbert Hoover. No picture of the life there more charmingly reveals the character of Alex Legge than does this incident recently related to the writer by Mr. Hoover:

"Alex Legge was greatly interested in the children of the village and did not fail to bring around a horde of them to get autographs each time I appeared. He seemed to have incurred obligations in this direction prior to my arrival. What was more, he appeared to have relations to the automobile of every boy who drove into the place. There was a procession of these youngsters coming to the steps and receiving mystic signs from Mr. Legge which entitled them to go to the garage and fill up with gas and oil.

"Two youngsters came in an old model T Ford minus its starting device. As they were unable to get the engine started by other means, Mr. Legge personally put the car into motion by pushing it.

"I talked with the boys owning this car and they explained that they could have secured one with a starting device for $6. Not having that much money, they bought the one that had to be pushed, paying $3.75 for it. Mr. Legge entered into the conversation at this point, saying that he would furnish the difference if they would turn in the $3.75 car against the $6 one. Apparently he was on personal terms with most of the children in the village and knew all about their various enterprises, being an active participant in many of them."

This was the Alex Legge who loved the youngsters— "the wee trooties," like Old Sandy, his father. Comradeship with the children of the community was one of his keenest pleasures.

There was a survival of the farm boy in Alex Legge. Apparently his only vanity took the form of showing off his great physical strength and endurance. In these displays he was sometimes a rough playmate. Men guests at the Legge estate were invariably invited to work on the farm. The favorite excuse was, "I'm sorry; but I have no suitable clothes with me." Mr. Legge would smile and reply that there was no need to worry about that as the hall closet was stocked with outfits of working clothes.

Cy Denman says: "Two incidents stand out in my memory which vividly illustrate Alex Legge's deep concern for those who were less fortunate than himself.

"He was engaged in building some cottages on the Memorial Farm where undernourished children were received for recuperation and special care. A family of several children had been sent to the first cottage sometime previous to my visit. They were playing in the nearby woods and he called them to the car. They were certainly a rosy-cheeked, lively crew. Then, proudly, he told me that, when they had arrived, they were weak and pale because their father, an ex-service man, had been unable to work for many months and could not supply them with milk and other special foods needed for their upbuilding. These were at once furnished them at the farm. I shall never forget the expression on his face when the children came bounding to the car.

"The other incident occurred the last time I visited him, just as we were ready to leave the farm for his Hinsdale house. Alex went to one of the storerooms and brought out two large tubs which he gave me to carry, while he carried a stepladder. I helped him fill these tubs with elderberries from high bushes. He explained that a charwoman at the office in town had told him that she wished she had some elderberries to make wine for her husband who was an invalid."

Mr. Legge was intensely interested in the 4-H Club movement. Four-H Clubs had had sproutings in various parts of the country as early as 1899. The National Committee was organized informally in 1919, and in December, 1921, the formal organization was completed and offices established.

Guy L. Noble, managing director of the National

Committee on Boys and Girls Club Work, approached Alex Legge in 1923 regarding this program.

"I went to his office and talked to him and he listened attentively. He then attended a meeting of our directors. At a point in the proceedings where it seemed that nothing was going to be done, Alex Legge suddenly said: 'Well, men, we haven't done anything for Noble and his farm boys and girls yet. Let's decide to help them out.'

"He saved the situation so far as I was concerned. A program was adopted, and he helped put it over."

Mr. Noble treasures a statement which Mr. Legge gave to him in 1924 regarding the Boys and Girls Club Work:

The economics of producing agricultural products at a less cost including the conservation of soil fertility, is the foundation of future agricultural prosperity. It is my judgment that more progress is being made in this line through the activities of the Boys and Girls Club work than through any other channel.

Mr. Legge attended every Directors' meeting that was called and even urged that additional metings be held to determine how the National Committee might further assist in the development of the 4-H program for farm boys and girls. He was a generous annual contributor to the work and very influential in securing support from other quarters. He originated the plan of entertaining the 4-H Club members in attendance at the annual International Live Stock Show and the National 4-H Club Congress. When he retired from the Federal Farm Board, the papers carried the following:

"In a statement immediately following his resignation as chairman of the Farm Board, on March 6, Alexander Legge recommended that more attention be given to the Boys and Girls Clubs, saying: 'I would also offer the suggestion that in the future more attention be given to the young folks, particularly the Boys and Girls Clubs, who in their competitive contests are learning the value of teamwork. It does not matter much what becomes of us old fellows who will soon be out of the picture. The problems of the future must be met by the coming generation.'"

Temperamentally, Alex Legge was not the typical modern organization man. He cut red tape at every opportunity. While he had a wholesome respect for written records, his natural impulse was to give oral rather than written instructions.

"In his earlier years," says an executive of the Harvester Company, "Mr. Legge had run his own errands. As administrator of company affairs, when he thought of some plan to be put into action he sprang to his feet and went to the person to whom he wished to assign a task. His tall figure was a familiar one in the hallways and corridors of the Harvester building, delivering in person to his associates the documents with which he wished them to deal. His promotion to the company presidency utterly failed to transform him into a secluded front-office executive who summoned others to appear before him. Evidently the machinery of business irritated him, for the volume of inter-office communications in writing from his desk was amazingly small considering the amount of work which he administered. Again, he was a sparing user of the telephone in communicating with his office associates. He preferred personal, face-to-face contact with them, feeling that he could get closer to any situation by this direct method that had been the habit of his life. Besides, he enjoyed talking with his associates and their callers.

"It became generally recognized that making 'preliminary' reports was decidedly an unsafe procedure. Mr. Legge wanted no reports on a partially investigated situation; all the vital facts must be reviewed in any report that met his approval."

A man in high position in the industrial world made this interesting comment on the peculiarities of Alex Legge's mental processes in reaching decisions involving diverse and complex elements and interests:

"The usual way of adjusting differences in such situations is by adroit compromise. But Mr. Legge arrived at a course of co-operative action in a way that was strikingly individual. Up to a certain point he listened silently to the conference table talk with his eyes closed to narrow slits and apparently somewhat bored by the proceedings. Suddenly, he would shoot a few sharp questions and then remark: 'It seems to me we have gone far enough with this to see what is chaff and what is wheat. It looks to me about this way.' Then he would pierce through the whole problem to its backbone, with all confusing considerations swept aside. With a few swift strokes he would sketch the course of action that appealed to him as being 'the common sense thing' to do.

"In my opinion Alex Legge had the most penetrating mind with which I have ever come in contact. That expression is not original with me, but it is sensitively descriptive. He had this gift in a measure that amounted to positive genius.

"In essence, it was an amazing capacity for reducing a large and complicated problem to its least common denominator. Abraham Lincoln had the same gift in affairs of statesmanship and politics. A part of this amazing gift in both these men was their clear, intuitive understanding of human nature. Both had the viewpoint of the

ALEXANDER LEGGE WHEN HE WAS CHAIRMAN OF THE FEDERAL FARM BOARD
(PHOTOGRAPH BY BACHRACH)

common man—the man on the farm, in the factory, in the store, and on the street! Intuitively, they knew the thoughts and the feelings of the great mass of Americans. In any problem that Alex Legge tackled he did not leave out the human equation."

CHAPTER

XVI

The Farm Foundation

1933

BY a gift of $400,000 in 1933 and a bequest of
$500,000 in his will, Alex Legge dedicated the
greater part of his estate to the improvement of
the life of the rural population of America. This disposi-
tion of the accumulations of his life work affords a measure of the depth and breadth and sincerity of his interest
in the well-being of American farmers.

Public announcement of the formation of the Farm
Foundation was delayed pending the enlargement of the
supporting group, and up to his death Mr. Legge worked
to this end as diligently as his other duties would permit.
His death and the publication of his will leaving a bequest to the Farm Foundation precipitated an announcement by Ex-Governor Frank O. Lowden of Illinois,
chairman of the Board of Trustees.

In February, 1933, a trust agreement was drawn up
creating the Farm Foundation. Alex Legge had been the
moving spirit in this project. As early as 1930, he had offered to match dollar for dollar any sum given by any
member of the United States Chamber of Commerce for
the purpose of experimentation in agriculture, saying:

"Men of wealth have left large fortunes for foundations and organizations of one kind or another to promote research in the fields of medicine, industry, mining and practically all the fields of science except agriculture. Men of wealth have left fortunes to support hospitals, art galleries and museums, but it is significant that practically all of the large fortunes have been left for educational, research and cultural activities that are largely available to the urban population. There is a place in America for a foundation to which men and women may leave their contributions that will be dedicated to the advancement of the rural people."

Ex-Governor Lowden's public announcement of the Farm Foundation said:

"For many years Mr. Legge had felt the need of some agency free from local or political considerations, which could act as a clearing house and testing ground of ideas for the improvement of farming conditions and farm life and encourage experimentation and co-operative effort along sound lines. Such an agency should be adequately endowed and equipped to carry on research and educational work and directed by trustees chosen for their diversified experience, recognized ability, and interest in farm problems.

"The same need was voiced in the report of the Business Men's Committee appointed in 1927 to study agricultural conditions, by joint action of the Chamber of Commerce of the United States and the National Industrial Conference Board.

"While Mr. Legge was developing interest in this plan, another group in New York in which Mrs. Mary Harriman Rumsey and George MacDonald were active, had reached the same conclusion.

"The result was the formation of an organization committee which formulated a plan along the lines suggested by Mr. Legge and the setting up of the Farm Foundation by execution of a trust agreement."

The trust agreement, describing the objects of the Foundation, says:

Recognizing the importance to the national welfare of improving and at all times maintaining healthy and satisfying conditions of life for the farming and rural population of the country with adequate economic returns and social, educational and cultural advantages, a continuing foundation to be known as the Farm Foundation is hereby created. . . .

1. To encourage and develop co-operative effort and community organization and consciousness as means for improving the economic, social, educational and cultural conditions of rural life.
2. To stimulate and conduct research and experimental work for the study of any economic, social, educational or scientific problem of importance to any substantial portion of the rural population of the country, including problems of production, marketing and purchasing and the sound co-ordination of the agricultural with the industrial, financial, and mercantile life of the country.
3. To encourage, aid or finance any university, institution, corporation or persons in the conduct of any such research or experimental work.
4. To disseminate educational and useful information developed as a result of any such study, research and experimentation, or otherwise, in such manner as to be of practical value to the farming population.
5. To promote and enlarge the intellectual and cultural interests and opportunities of the rural population through community action.

Mr. Legge gave much thought to the provisions of the trust agreement creating the Farm Foundation and particularly to the setting up of some plan which would insure an active and well-balanced board of trustees not only for the present, but for the distant future. He did not want the Foundation to go to seed. The trust agreement provides that no trustee shall serve for over ten years. It also provides for classification of the twenty-one trustees as follows:

Five members experienced in and representing farming.

Three members from the executive, teaching, experimental or extension staffs of three Land Grant Universities or State Universities maintaining agricultural departments.

Six members, one each chosen as experienced in and representing finance, manufacture, merchandising, transportation, the farm press, and radio as a means of education.

Seven members at large.

The members of the first board of trustees named in the Foundation agreement were:

Farmer Members: Frank O. Lowden, Charles C. Teague, Roy Johnson, W. E. Riegel, R. E. Lambert

Finance Member: Melvin A. Traylor

Manufacturing Member: Owen D. Young

Merchant Member: Robert E. Wood

Transportation Member: Ralph Budd

Farm Press Member: Dan A. Wallace

Radio Member: Frank E. Mullen

University Members: Chris L. Christensen, A. R. Mann, F. D. Farrell

Members at large: Bernard M. Baruch, Alexander Legge, George MacDonald, Clarence Poe, Mary Harriman Rumsey, John Stuart, Clifford V. Gregory

The Foundation is permanent and it is the hope of the founders that it may become a helpful factor, contributing over the years to the solution of problems affecting the welfare of the farming and rural population of our country. Its field, which is not duplicated by any other existing foundation, is broad, covering any social, educational, economic or cultural problems of interest to any substantial portion of the rural population and including the sound co-ordination of the agricultural life of the country with its urban and industrial life.

XVII

The End of the Trail
1933

DURING the latter part of November, 1933, Carl
Williams spent a week-end at Hinsdale with
Mr. Legge.

"He was cheerful as always," says Mr. Williams, "but
evidently failing. I was censuring some of the laws which
had been put into effect. Alex responded: 'Oh, sit tight
in the boat. Praise where you can; say nothing where you
can't approve. It'll all come out in the wash.' To me,
that last remark expresses Alex Legge; he firmly believed
that 'God's in His Heaven' and that it would all come out
in the wash."

One week to a day before his death, Alex Legge went
to Dane County, Wisconsin, and visited the scenes of his
childhood in the company of his friend Leo Lunenschloss, who looked after his personal interests there.
While Mr. Legge gave many instructions regarding the
purchase of the Elder farm and the development of other
property which he already owned, he was in a pensive,
retrospective mood. Every place intimately associated
with his childhood was visited and he related to his com-

panion why each particular spot stood out in his memory. They called upon many of his old friends and talked with them about his people and the incidents and circumstances of their lives.

It was not a happy pilgrimage for Mr. Lunenschloss who later said: "It seemed to me that Mr. Legge had an intuition that this was destined to be his last pilgrimage to the haunts of his childhood. While he spoke of plans for the future, his mood was dreamy and sad. He showed pathetic weariness, physical weakness. A few days after he left me he was dead."

Saturday morning, December 2, he spent at the office, working on the code for the agricultural machinery industry. Arch W. Shaw, who had been his friend since the War Industries Board days, visited with him that morning. He says:

"My son and I stopped in at the office, intending to stay but a few minutes. I had learned from experience to be expeditious in any business which I had with him.

"He said he was tired, and lay back in his big chair and put his feet on the table. He kept talking about the NRA and how much he had to do and how tired he was. No matter what the momentary subject of conversation was, it always wound up with the NRA and the codes, as though the pressure of that problem rested heavily on him.

"We were there an hour and a half, and had to be rather insistent when we left. It seemed as though he didn't want us to leave—as though he wanted someone there with him."

That evening, former Secretary of Agriculture Hyde called Mr. Legge on the telephone. "When I asked him how he felt he said, 'I never felt better physically nor worse mentally' and referred to the enormous amount of work he had been doing on the codes. But of course he was the kind of man who would never admit he was below par physically, no matter how he felt."

Alex Legge had invited eleven friends to dinner on Sunday, and had written Mr. Noble that he would attend the annual meeting of the National Committee on Boys and Girls Club work on Monday.

On Saturday, he drove out to Hinsdale, taking Mr. W. M. Gale with him as a week-end guest. Early Sunday morning he went out to his beloved Memorial Farm. He started setting out some lilacs in the garden. At ten o'clock he felt so ill that he telephoned Dr. James A. Britton, his close friend and the company's chief medical officer, asking him to come out at once.

His symptoms rapidly grew more alarming and he was taken to his home in Hinsdale and a neighborhood doctor was called. At 11:15 a.m., before either of the physicians had arrived, Alex Legge passed away. Death was pronounced due to the forming of a blood clot near the heart. That was December 3, 1933.

The entire world was shocked by the news of Mr. Legge's passing. From almost every section of the globe came cables, wires and letters. In the offices of the Harvester Company is a book containing facsimiles of all the messages received. These communications from intimates, friends, business associates and mere acquaintances are testimonials of the love they felt toward this kindly, unspoiled, great American.

One of the most poignant of these is an unsigned letter, mailed at Paris, Missouri, entitled "A Simple Tribute to a Great Man—Mr. Legge":

Your work is done; you have passed on to that distant vale. That which is mortal can remain only for a short time, but the immortal spark, the work of the truly great, can never be quenched by time or decay.

Though occupying one of the greatest positions in the world of business, with responsibilities and cares enough to crush many men, you found the time, you understood, you sympathized with an unemployed young man practically unknown to you. You helped, you inspired, you renewed a determination during days of distressing unemployment, periods of uncertainty such as our great nation has never heretofore experienced. What you would do for one you would do for all.

There are letters from 4-H boys and girls, from the children of the community, from boyhood friends, and from all ranks of Harvester employees. Side by side with these are wires and letters from men occupying the highest places in the nation—financiers, economists, educators, physicians, agriculturists, diplomats—all sorrowful because their good friend Alex Legge had passed on. Testimonials from the Chicago Club, the Commercial Club, the Chicago Athletic Club and the Congressional Club of Washington; also from the Chicago Association of Commerce, the Harvester Board of Directors, and various works councils of the Harvester Company.

Because it was impossible for the great number of people wishing to attend the last rites for Mr. Legge to be accommodated in the Union Church at Hinsdale, services were held at the Fourth Presbyterian Church at 880 North Michigan Avenue, Chicago, on December 6. Rev. Harrison Ray Anderson was in charge, with Rev. Wilfred A. Rowell of Hinsdale assisting.

The active pallbearers were:

A. A. Jones	C. R. McDonald
George W. Koenig	John Morrow, Jr.
J. L. McCaffrey	George E. Rose
Fowler McCormick	A. W. Scarratt

The honorary pallbearers were:

Bernard M. Baruch
Cassius F. Biggert
Ralph Budd
John A. Chapman
Chris L. Christensen
Thomas E. Donnelley
William S. Elliott
William M. Gale
John J. Glessner
Carl Gray
Maurice F. Holahan
Dr. D. B. Holcomb
Horace H. Holcomb
Herbert Hoover
Arthur M. Hyde
Hugh S. Johnson

Edward A. Johnston
Arnold B. Keller
Frank B. Kellogg
William P. Kelly
John A. Kratz
James R. Leavell
Frank O. Lowden
Sydney G. McAllister
Chauncey McCormick
Cyrus McCormick
Cyrus H. McCormick
Harold F. McCormick
Charles H. MacDowell
Samuel R. McKelvie
Addis E. McKinstry
Donald R. McLennan

Eugene Meyer, Jr.
Arthur F. Mullen
George N. Peek
Herbert F. Perkins
George A. Ranney
William M. Reay
Stanley Reed
Henry M. Robinson
Daniel C. Roper
James C. Stone
Judson F. Stone
John Stuart
Melvin A. Traylor
Sanford B. White
John P. Wilson

In the course of his simple eulogy, Dr. Rowell quoted this tribute of Cyrus H. McCormick's:

"In our active and arduous life with its modern influences, there appears at long intervals a man who is a character so different from the ordinary that we see in him a man of the olden type, who has lifted himself far above the levels of average humanity. In him we see a man so simple and direct in his bearing, so modest in his nature, so unconventional in his relation to others, so honest in his statements, so strong and rugged in his character that he impresses us as being a leader of men to be admired, respected, and followed. Such a man was Abraham Lincoln; such a man was Robert E. Lee of Virginia; such a man was Alexander Legge who has just left us for the Great Beyond."

Alex Legge inspired a very unusual affection in those who knew him. Mr. Baruch, who came to Chicago for the funeral of his dear friend, and made a second trip from the East when Alex Legge's ashes were taken to the

Katherine Legge Memorial to be interred beside those of his beloved wife, sent the following wire upon being notified of Mr. Legge's death:

"Wise and unselfish in council, fearless in thought and action, unflinchingly loyal to his friends and to the highest of ideals, gentle and tender, always thoughtful and solicitous of the disadvantaged and unhappy, ever mindful of and responsive to his obligations and duties as a citizen and an American, we shall not soon see his like again. In the meeting place of the souls of the truly great there will be welcomed as an equal the one we have been privileged to know so well and love so much."

Although no members of his family of his generation were left to mourn him, his three nephews, Roy Legge of San Francisco, Alex E. Legge and James Legge of Rogers, Nebraska, and three nieces, Miss Ina Sharman and Mrs. Helen Creelman of San Diego, and Mrs. Mildred Gossett of San Francisco, felt an irreparable loss in the passing of this uncle for whom family ties, whether near or distant, had always been strong and enduring.

For many years, Mr. Legge had left his personal affairs entirely in the hands of his good friend William M. Gale, and Mr. Gale and Mr. George A. Ranney were appointed co-executors of the estate.

No finer tribute could be given any man than that by Harold F. McCormick, entitled "In Memoriam," which was published in the January-February, 1934, edition of the *Harvester World*:

"His younger days on the frontier gave his nature the food that makes strength of soul, and the many long periods of solitude gave him opportunities for reflection and the development of self-reliance; and the primitive life of the plains was like a crucible of character, turning the native iron of his integrity and resoluteness into steel of proof, and bringing out his finest and deepest qualities —honesty, fearlessness, sagacity.

"Notwithstanding all his hard self-schooling and his endless grappling with difficult circumstance, no tinge of cynicism or skepticism or expediency ever affected his innate tenderness of heart, or kept him from putting out a helping hand to his fellow man, or disturbed his serenity and poise. However stern he might need to be upon occasion as a commander, he was always harder upon himself than upon any other man. No right-thinking, right-doing man ever had occasion to fear him, yet none ever dared to take liberties with his deeper reserves of dignity. Toward him affectionate admiration and true respect always went hand in hand.

"Essentially simple in all his tastes, and frankly indifferent as to externals, yet he wore a rich invisible mantle of personality, shining and splendid.

"In council he was patient, conciliatory, an eloquent listener, with a special ability for drawing out and harmonizing divergent points of view. In administration he always had and used a firmness of ultimate decision; and once he had charted a course that he knew to be true, he held to it straight as an arrow. To others he freely accorded the credit that was their due, and for himself he was content to assume full responsibility for any unforeseen and untoward condition or circumstance that might arise.

"Alex Legge was in his home life a devoted husband, in all his relations a loyal friend, and in the associations of business an inspiring co-worker and a great leader.

"His life work, following to the very last a chosen course from which none could cause him to depart, has come to an end, but the remembrance of association with him and of his leadership will remain a living thing, bright and cherished."

All who knew Alex Legge are agreed that he was one of the simplest men who ever achieved international influence and fame. His world was wholly inhabited by "folks," unseparated into social strata. His mental processes were as direct as the rays of the sun. His honesty was elemental and profound, unwarped by devious thinking. His courage of opinion and performance made him one of the most notable individualists of his time. He was human to the core and abounded in tenderness and sympathy. His concepts of justice were liberal—rarely so for the administrator of a vast business. The bonds of family attachment were strong in him; he provided generously for the future of all his kin while he was living—and he gave them more than money.

The patriotism of Alex Legge never encountered a sincere challenge. In the service of his country he was as single-minded as he was devoted and his official acts were not controlled by consideration of his private interests; often they were in direct opposition to his personal advantage. He was internationally-minded in the broadest and finest sense of the term. His training as the leading spirit of a great industrial organization doing business in virtually all parts of the world had given him this viewpoint.

Love for the people of the soil was his dominant attachment. This was attested by his great bequest to the Farm Foundation for the continued study, throughout the years, of the farmers' problems. The progress of American agriculture was his controlling interest when he drew up his will.

His ability to inspire the loyalty and affection of those with whom he worked or was associated was phenomenal and few men have enjoyed this devotion in equal degree.

Alex Legge was as truly the Abraham Lincoln of Agriculture as of Industry.

THE LAKESIDE PRESS

R. R. DONNELLEY & SONS COMPANY

CHICAGO, ILLINOIS

1936